CONTEMPORARY ENGLISH
BOOK 2

Jeanne Becijos

Mechelle Perrott

Cecelia Ryan

CB

CONTEMPORARY BOOKS

a division of NTC/CONTEMPORARY PUBLISHING GROUP
Lincolnwood, Illinois USA

Project Manager: Roseanne Mendoza
Cover Illustration: Regan Dunnick
Interior Illustrations: Regan Dunnick, Amanda Duffy, Jean Wisenbaugh

Acknowledgments

The authors and publisher would like to thank the following people for their help
and contribution to *Contemporary English:*
Series Consultant: **Catherine Porter,** Adult Learning Resource Center, Des Plaines, Illinois.
Reviewers: **Lisa Agao,** Resource Teacher, Fresno Adult School, Clovis, CA; **Bea Berrettini,**
Instructor, Fresno Adult School, Fresno, CA; **Lemuel S. Bonilla,** Professor, ESL, Santiago
Canyon College, Costa Mesa, CA; **Janice Bruno,** Instructor/Resource Teacher, Fresno Adult
School, Fresno, CA; **Mary Lou Byrne,** ESL Director, Triton College, River Grove, IL;
Clíf de Córdoba, Assistant Principal, Southgate Community Adult School, Los Angeles, CA;
Jill DeGrange, ESL Program Director, Salinas Adult School, Salinas, CA; **Samuela Eckstut,**
Senior Lecturer, CELOP, Boston University, Melrose, MA; **Stephen Ewert,** Instructor, Fresno
Adult School, Fresno, CA; **Eric Glicker,** Instructor, Rancho Santiago Community College District,
Santa Ana, CA; **Joyce Halenar,** Instructor/Advisor, Salinas Adult School, Salinas, CA; **Mary Jahr-
Purvis,** ESL Teacher, Salinas Adult School, Salinas, CA; **Robert Jenkins,** Assistant Professor,
Centennial Education Center, Santa Ana College, Santa Ana, CA; **Ruth Luman,** Instructor,
Long Beach Adult School, Long Beach, CA; **Sue Mendizza,** Coordinator, School of Continuing
Education, Santa Ana College, Santa Ana, CA; **Rachel Porcelli,** Independent Consultant, Dade
County, FL; **John Richardson,** Instructor, Fresno Adult School, Fresno, CA; **Judy Rosselli,**
VESL Instructor, San Diego Community College District, San Diego, CA; **Sandra Saldana,**
Lead Instructor, ESL Program, Triton College, River Grove, IL; **Kay Taggart,** Curriculum
Coordinator, Literacy and Workforce Development Center, El Paso Community College, El Paso,
TX; **Abigail H. Tom,** Instructor, Durham Technical Community College, Durham, NC.

Special thanks to **Jan Jarrell,** ESL Department Chair, Cesar Chavez Center, San Diego
Community College District, San Diego, CA, and **Donna Price Machado,** VESL Lab Coordinator,
San Diego Community College District, San Diego, CA; Steve Gwyne and Cathren Bouldin
at Mid-City Continuing Education Center, San Diego, CA.

The authors appreciate the following students, family members and friends for allowing them
to include stories from their lives: Cassdeail E. Brown, Verner Elizondo, Jon and Alice Fredricks,
Maggie Hamidi, Julio Cesar Osorio, Hien Pham, and Juan Toj.

We lovingly dedicate this book to our family members, Ron and Ryan Becijos, Gina Catania,
and Per Martin, and to our elegant editor, Roseanne Mendoza.

ISBN: 0-8092-0704-4

Published by Contemporary Books,
a division of NTC/Contemporary Publishing Group, Inc.

CONTENTS

ABOUT THIS SERIES

PROGRAM COMPONENTS AND PHILOSOPHY

Contemporary English is a five-level interactive topic-based English-as-a-Second-Language series for adult learners ranging from the beginning-literacy level to the high-intermediate level. The series includes

- Student Books for classroom use

- Workbooks (Book 1–Book 4) for independent use at home, in the classroom, or in a lab

- Audiocassettes for individual student, classroom, or lab use and

- Teacher's Manuals, with reproducible activity masters and unit progress checks for assessment.

These materials were correlated from inception to the California Model Standards for Adult ESL Programs, the MELT Student Performance Levels, and the SCANS (Secretary's Commission on Achieving Necessary Skills) Competencies.

Unique among adult ESL series, *Contemporary English* presents high-interest topics as a framework for developing a wide variety of language, thinking, and life skills. In addition to focusing on listening, speaking, reading, and writing skills, *Contemporary English* integrates work on language structures; problem-solving, critical-thinking, and graphic-literacy skills; and—increasingly important—work-related skills.

Contemporary English empowers students to take charge of their learning and to develop strong communication skills for the real world. For example, each unit in Books 1–4 falls under one of the following broad topics: Home and Neighborhood, People and Machines, Employment and Opportunity, Human Relations, Consumer Economics, Community Services, Transportation and Travel, Healthy Living, History and Geography, and Arts and Entertainment. (The lowest-level book, *Contemporary English* Literacy, addresses all of these topics except History and Geography and, Arts and Entertainment.) In short, the series addresses topics of interest and concern to adult learners.

Contemporary English presents engaging and meaningful situations that provide a context for grammar structures, listening activities, and an emphasis on the world of work. Within this framework each unit offers a wealth of pair and group activities, often with designated team roles, and frequent individual and group presentations to the class. This approach mirrors the team organization characteristic of today's workplace and reflects the recent influence on education of the Department of Labor's SCANS report.

UNIT STRUCTURE OF THE STUDENT BOOKS

Contemporary English provides a controlled and predictable sequence of instruction and activities. Conveniently for teachers, each page of a unit functions as a self-contained mini-lesson. Each unit is divided into two parts, each of which begins with a **Scene** that presents, in comic-strip format, incidents from the lives of newcomers to the United States or aspects of U.S. culture that students encounter regularly. Lively, humorous, and dramatic, the **Scenes** engage students in the unit topics—usually by presenting typical problems in the lives of average people. A series of discussion questions proceeds from factual comprehension of the **Scene** to personalization and, in Books 3 and 4, problem solving.

After each opening **Scene** comes **Sound Bites,** a focused listening task that includes pre-listening and post-listening work. **Sound Bites** presents target content and language structures through lively conversations and other samples of natural speech, such as telephone answering-machine messages and transportation announcements.

Throughout *Contemporary English*, grammar structures are first contextualized in the **Scenes** and listening activities and then presented, practiced, and applied on follow-up **Spotlight** pages. Appearing two to four times in each unit, the **Spotlight** pages model target structures in contexts related to the unit topic. Special **Spotlight** feature boxes present the target structures schematically and provide brief, straightforward explanations when necessary. Exercises following the structure presentations allow students to manipulate the structures in meaningful contexts, such as stories or real-life situations. **Spotlight** pages usually end with a **Your Turn** and/or **In Your Experience** activity providing communicative application of the new structures.

These last two features, in addition to **Vocabulary Prompts,** occur within the units at the point of need, rather than in a fixed or unvarying part of each unit. **Vocabulary Prompts,** for example, serves to isolate challenging vocabulary before a listening or reading task. **Your Turn,** a follow-up to reading, listening, or structure practice, serves as a participatory task. **In Your Experience,** an activity drawing on students' prior knowledge and personal lives, allows learners to personalize the topics and relate them to their own experience.

Listening and speaking skills are developed further in the **Person to Person** activities, which present recorded two-person conversations exploring the unit topics in natural, colloquial language. Students listen to conversations, practice them, and work in pairs to complete a final open-ended dialogue. Students can then present their new conversations to the class.

Contemporary English helps students develop their reading skills and become motivated readers of English through **Reading for Real,** a page in each unit that provides stimulating authentic or adapted texts. With passages and realia that typically relate directly to the lives of characters in the **Scenes, Reading for Real** includes such real-life documents as a winning job résumé, instructions for office voice mail, biographies of real people, advice from the local police, and listings of music festivals around the country. Follow-up activities (such as **Your Turn** and **In Your Experience**) extend and personalize the reading.

Culture Corner provides further work on reading skills by focusing on the useful inside information about U.S. life that students love. Presented as brief readings typically paired with charts, graphics, or artwork, **Culture Corner** gives students the information they need to adapt to a culture that can often be confusing and difficult to understand. Interactive follow-up activities help students integrate cultural knowledge with their language skills.

Graphic literacy is the focus of **Get Graphic,** a feature that offers practice in reading charts, graphs, diagrams, and timelines—skills that are crucial in the workplace and for preparing for the GED. **Get Graphic** provides high-interest stimuli related to the unit topics and characters while it incorporates or recycles target language structures. A typical feature of this page is a follow-up activity in which learners develop their own simple graphs or charts and share them with partners or groups. The activities on this page help students learn to read, interpret, and use information in a graphic format.

Problem-solving and critical-thinking skills are developed further in **Issues and Answers**. This feature typically presents two opinions—often in direct opposition—in formats such as advice columns or letters to the editor. **Issues and Answers** contains short, humorous texts with views of U.S. life from a variety of perspectives, including those of immigrants and their "cultural advisors"—the experts who help to orient the newcomers as they bridge the gap between their native and adopted countries.

The last page of each unit contains a **Wrap-Up,** a project in which students use a graphic organizer such as a T-chart, a Venn diagram, an idea map, or a timeline to brainstorm and organize ideas and then talk or write in a group. Following **Wrap-Up** is the self-assessment activity **Think About Learning,** a final reflection task that asks students to evaluate the quality of their own learning on the major content points, life skills, and language structures in the unit. Students can thus assess what they have learned and provide feedback to the teacher, all of which helps to build a learner-centered classroom.

ABOUT BOOK 2

Book 2 focuses on family and neighborhood, community resources, consumer economics in the United States, specific career options, and job skills for the new workplace. Careful linguistic support allows learners to tackle these sophisti- cated unit topics. Throughout each unit, students simultaneously learn key employment skills such as working with a team and monitoring themselves for errors while they absorb useful background content on U.S. culture.

ICONS

Contemporary English uses the following six icons throughout the series:

 Listening—All conversations and other speech samples are recorded on tape.

 Speaking—Students speak with a partner, a group, or the class.

 Reading—Students read a passage, a graphic, or a short text.

 Writing—Students write letters, words, or phrases.

 Critical Thinking—Students perform an activity that requires critical-thinking skills.

 Spotlight—Students complete an exercise that provides practice on the structures presented on the **Spotlight** page. These exercises may require a variety of language skills, but structure practice is the principal focus of the exercise.

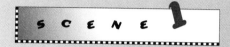

Talk about the pictures with a partner.
Ask each other the questions below.
Share your answers with another pair or the class.

Mario and Tam are on the city bus.

FACTS Where are the two men? Where are they going?

FEELINGS Which man feels old? Which man probably feels young?

AND YOU? Do you know some young students in your school?
Do you know some older students?
What age is too old for school?

VOCABULARY PROMPTS

Before you listen, talk with a partner about the words in the chart
of schools in the United States.

SCHOOL			GRADE		AGE
preschool					2 to 4 years old
elementary school			kindergarten		5 years old
			1st	first grade	6 years old
			2nd	second grade	7 years old
			3rd	third grade	8 years old
			4th	fourth grade	9 years old
			5th	fifth grade	10 years old
			6th	sixth grade	11 years old
middle		junior	7th	seventh grade	12 years old
			8th	eighth grade	13 years old
senior high school			9th	ninth grade	14 years old
			10th	tenth grade	15 years old
			11th	eleventh grade	16 years old
			12th	twelfth grade	17 years old
adult school	vocational school	university / college			18 to 100+ years old

SOUND BITES

Listen to people answering questions about a family member
or a roommate in school.

While You Listen Write the correct school, grade, and age in the chart.

NAME	STUDENT	SCHOOL	GRADE	AGE
1. Chela	son	elementary	1st	6
2. Mohammed	wife			
3. Lin	daughter			
4. Francisco	roommate			

After You Listen Check your answers with your partner.

Your Turn

With your partner make sentences about your answers. For example, say, "Chela
has a son. He is in elementary school. He is in the first grade. He is 6 years old."

In Your Experience

Talk with your partner about the schools, grades, and ages
of your family and friends.

SPOTLIGHT ON *Be* IN AFFIRMATIVE AND NEGATIVE STATEMENTS AND IN QUESTIONS

Affirmative

I **am**   a student.

I'**m**

He/She/It **is**   11 years old.

He'**s**/She'**s**/It'**s**

You/We/They **are**   in adult school

You'**re**/We'**re**/They'**re**

Negative

I **am not** a student.

I'**m not**

He/She/It **is not** 11 years old.

He'**s**/She'**s**/It'**s not**

You/We/They **are not**   in adult school.

You'**re**/We'**re**/They'**re not**

Questions

Statement:	Tam **is** a student.	They **are** students.
Question:	**Is** Tam a student?	**Are** they students?

In a question, the verb *be (am, is, are)* comes at the beginning.

Short Answers

Affirmative	**Negative**
Yes, I **am**.	No, I'**m not**.
Yes, he/she/it **is**.	No, he/she/it **isn't**.
Yes, you/we/they **are**.	No, you/we/they **aren't**.

There are two forms for *is not* and *are not*:

She'**s** not.	=	She **isn't**.
They'**re** not.	=	They **aren't**.

Exercise 1: Use the school chart from page 2 to help you answer questions about students in U.S. schools.

1. Karen is 14 years old. Is she in 9th grade? _____ Yes, she is _____.

2. John is in 12th grade. Is he in middle school? _____.

3. Lynn is 8 years old. Is she in 3rd grade? _____.

4. Bobby and Ken are 5 years old. Are they in kindergarten? _____.

5. Tam is 70 years old. Is he in adult school? _____.

6. Is the 10th grade for 10-year-old children? _____.

Person to Person

Talk to a partner about the signs. Then listen to the conversations.
Write a sentence to finish the last conversation.
Practice the conversations with your partner.

ROOM 258

LANGUAGE LAB

Open Hours: 8:00 A.M. to 9:00 A.M.
Noon to 1:00 P.M.
3:30 P.M. to 5:00 P.M.

STUDENT: Excuse me. Is the language lab open?

TEACHER: No, it isn't. It opens at 8:00.

STUDENT: Thanks.

Citizenship

Enroll now!
Free Classes!

STUDENT: Are you the teacher?

TEACHER: Yes, I am. Are you a new student?

STUDENT   No, I'm not. My mother wants to be a U.S. citizen. Can she enroll tomorrow?

Welcome Parents
OPEN HOUSE
Wilson Elementary School
Mrs. White's 6th Grade Class

MR. HASSAN: Hello. Are you Mrs. White?

MRS. WHITE: Yes, I am.

MR. HASSAN: I'm Ali Hassan, Sara's father.

MRS. WHITE: Nice to meet you. I'm happy so many of the students' parents are here!

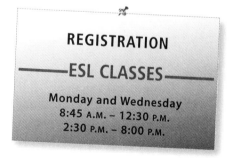

REGISTRATION

—— ESL CLASSES ——

Monday and Wednesday
8:45 A.M. – 12:30 P.M.
2:30 P.M. – 8:00 P.M.

STUDENT: Excuse me. Is registration for English classes here?

TEACHER: Yes, it is, but we're closed for lunch. Please come back at 2:30 P.M.

STUDENT: Oh, I can't today. Are you open Tuesday?

TEACHER: _____

In small groups talk about the meaning of the words below.

employees   pay increase   test   pass   supervisor   assembler

READING FOR REAL

Mario reads a sign at work.

EVANSTON ELECTRONICS

Computer Classes

Beginning next week, assemblers can go to computer classes on Tuesdays and Thursdays from 3:30 P.M. to 5:30 P.M.

Employees need to pass a computer test to get a pay increase.

See your supervisor to start.

1201 Commerce Road   Los Angeles, CA 90210

Exercise 2: With your group answer these questions about the sign.

1. Who can go to classes at Evanston Electronics?
2. What kind of classes are they?
3. When are the classes?
4. Why is it good to pass the test?
5. Who does an employee see to start classes?

Talk About It

 Can people often go to class at work? On the bus Mario says he's too old for school. Do you think he will sign up for the class? Why or why not?

In Your Experience

Ask a partner these questions.

Do you have a job? What kind of job do you have?
Do your friends and family have jobs? What jobs do they have?
Do you go to class at your job? Can you use a computer?

CULTURE CORNER

In small groups talk about the two pictures. What are the people saying? Why?

Please say that again.

Please speak more slowly.

Speaking Up: Say Something When You Don't Understand!

In the United States it's OK to ask questions when you don't understand something. Teachers like students to ask questions when they don't understand. On a job your boss or supervisor wants you to ask questions too. Supervisors sometimes get angry when employees don't understand but don't ask questions.

Exercise 3: Below are six expressions to use when you don't understand. Use the words in the list to complete the expressions.

pardon   understand   excuse   say   speak   repeat

1. ___Excuse___ me?   4. _____ me?

2. Please _____ that again.   5. I'm sorry. I don't _____ .

3. Please _____ more slowly.   6. Would you _____ that, please?

Your Turn

With a partner read each conversation two or three times.
Try to use all the expressions above in each conversation.

TEACHER:	Take out a paper. Write your name at the top.
STUDENT:	_____
TEACHER:	I said take out a paper and write your name at the top.
STUDENT:	Thanks. I understand now.

BOSS:	Please take this box to Barb Brown.
EMPLOYEE:	_____
BOSS:	I said take this to Barbara Brown.
EMPLOYEE:	No problem. I'll go right away.

Ha, a new student, comes to Tam's class. This is her first day in school in the United States.

FACTS   What do you see in the first picture?
What do you see in the second picture?

FEELINGS   How does Ha feel about her new classroom, happy or confused?

AND YOU?   Which classroom is like schools in your country?

 ## SOUND BITES

Ha and some classmates are talking in a group in class.

Before You Listen   In a group talk about the pictures.

happy   sad   confused   angry   tired

While You Listen   How does each speaker feel? Circle *a* or *b*
for the speaker's feelings.

1. Ha   2. Leonor   3. Francisco

a   b   a   b   a   b

4. Tam   5. Chela

a   b   a   b

After You Listen   Share your answers with a partner.

SPOTLIGHT ON PAST OF BE

Statements	Negatives	Contractions
I **was** happy.	I **was not** sad.	I **wasn't** sad.
You **were** tired.	You **were not** sad.	You **weren't** sad.
She / He **was** angry.	She / He **was not** sad.	She / He **wasn't** sad.
It **was** good.	It **was not** good.	It **wasn't** good.
We **were** happy.	We **were not** sad.	We **weren't** sad.
They **were** happy.	They **were not** sad.	They **weren't** sad.

Questions

Were we / you / they happy?

Was she / he happy?

Was it good?

Short Answers

Yes, I **was.** Yes, we / they **were.**

Yes, she / he **was.**

Yes, it **was.**

Exercise 4: Write sentences with *be* and the words below.
Use each word only once. Then check your answers with a partner.
In some cases several answers are possible.

happy	proud	worried	surprised	embarrassed
angry	sad	confused	tired	afraid

1. Leonor started work early yesterday. She _____ was tired _____.

2. Sara is a good student. Last week she showed
   her good report card to Mohammed and Jamila. They _____.

3. John met a new student yesterday.
   The student was 85 years old. John _____.

4. Last month Mario needed more money. He had many bills. He _____.

5. Yesterday in school Francisco had no pencil and no paper. He _____.

Your Turn

In your notebook write three more sentences about you or your classmates.
Use the three extra words above.

Person to Person

Listen to the conversation. Practice it with a partner.
Then change it to be true for you.

FRANCISCO: How are you doing in your new class?

HA: Fine. It's good this week. Last week I was confused.
But now I ask questions when I don't understand.

FRANCISCO: Good. You're going to learn fast.

SPOTLIGHT ON THE POSSESSIVE

Julie and Kathy are Ellen's daughters. = Ellen has two daughters, Julie and Kathy.

Singular Possessive

Mrs. White's 6th-grade class (Mrs. White has a 6th-grade class.)

Sara's father (Sara has a father.)

Plural Possessive

The students' parents (The students have parents.)

The teachers' students (The teachers have students.)

Note: The singular and plural have the same pronunciation but different spellings.

(Singular: **'s** Plural: **s'**).

The possessive sounds the same as the contraction of *is*. Listen carefully for the meaning.

Exercise 5: Complete the sentences below with the possessive form of the bold words.

1. **Mrs. White** teaches 6th grade. ____Mrs. White's____ class is in Room 10.

2. **Jan** has a new car. _____ car is the one in front of the building.

3. **The new students** were in school yesterday. _____ next class is tomorrow.

4. **The teachers** were in the office an hour ago. But _____ classes are just starting, so now they're in their classrooms.

5. **Sara** has classes in the morning. _____ classes start at 9:00.

6. **The parents** were with the teachers, and _____ children were outside the school.

Your Turn

Talk to a partner. Tell your partner about someone you know in school. Tell about that person's classes, school, or teacher. Use the possessive. For example, say, "My friend Salar's English classes are in the evening. Salar's teacher is from Washington, D.C., and the school is near his house."

GET GRAPHIC

The graph below is a pie graph.
What does it show?

THE AGE OF STUDENTS AT CITY CENTER ADULT SCHOOL

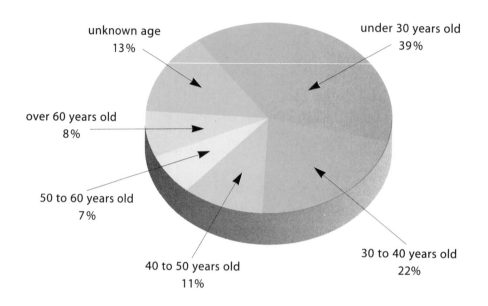

unknown age
13%

under 30 years old
39%

over 60 years old
8%

50 to 60 years old
7%

40 to 50 years old
11%

30 to 40 years old
22%

Exercise 6: There are 100 students of all ages at City Center Adult School.
Complete the sentences about the ages of students.

1. There are ___39___ students under 30 years old.

2. There are _____ students between 30 and 40 years old.

3. There are _____ students between 40 and 50 years old.

4. There are 7 students between _____ and _____ years old.

5. There are 8 students over _____ years old.

6. _____ students didn't give their ages.

 In Your Experience

How old are the students in your class?
Ask all the students, but remember—some people don't want to say their age.
It's a secret. How many are under 30? How many are between 30 and 40?
How many are between 50 and 60? How many are over 60?
How many don't want to say?

ISSUES AND ANSWERS

Read the letters below. If you don't know a word, ask your teacher. Then write a response to "Afraid."

Ask ABDUL and ANITA

DEAR ABDUL,

Why do teachers want students to work in small groups? I don't like to. I want to speak and listen to the teacher. I don't want to talk to other students!

CONFUSED

DEAR CONFUSED,

Your teacher is preparing you for the world outside school. Speaking and listening in small groups is good practice for talking to people at your job, at your children's school, and in your community. Your teacher is right—small groups give you good practice.

ABDUL

DEAR ANITA,

I have a problem. I'm a new student in class. The students don't speak my language. I want to have friends, but I am shy. What can I do?

AFRAID

DEAR AFRAID,

_____

_____

_____

_____

_____

_____

ANITA

In small groups share your answers to "Afraid."
Are your answers the same or different?

In Your Experience

Answer the questions below in your group. Talk about your answers.

Do you like working in small groups? Why or why not?

How many classmates speak your language?

WRAP-UP

This is an idea map. It helps you to think and organize your ideas.
The circle in the middle is the main idea, or topic.
The other circles are ideas about the topic. With a group finish the idea map.
Fill in all the circles you can.

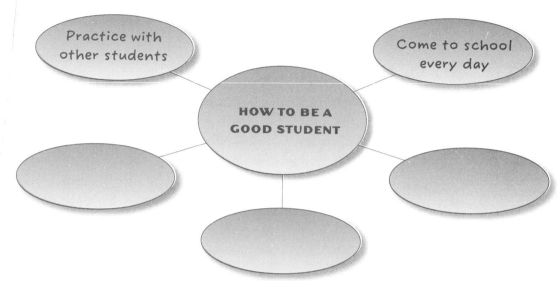

Practice with other students

Come to school every day

HOW TO BE A GOOD STUDENT

With your group make a list of your ideas. Organize your group's ideas.
Write important ideas first. Share your list with other groups.

Think About Learning

In this unit you learned a variety of skills and language structures.
Look at the items in the list below and check how easy or difficult each
was for you. At the bottom write one other thing you learned.

SKILLS / STRUCTURES	Page	easy ☺	so-so 😐	difficult ☹
Understand and talk about U.S. schools	2			
Listen to conversations about school	2			
Read and understand a sign at work	5			
Read a pie graph	10			
Read about and solve problems	11			
Use an idea map	12			
Ask and answer questions using *be*	3			
Ask and answer questions using the past of *be*	8			
Use 's to show possession	9			

Talk about the pictures with a partner.
Ask each other the questions below.
Share your answers with another pair or the class.

Janet and Chan are ready to leave work.

> What do you do to relax?

> I watch TV or read a magazine. Sometimes I listen to the radio.

> Janet, I need you in my office. We have two more hours of work.

> Finally! It's 5:00. I need to relax. What a day!

> Two more hours? Tonight? All right.

FACTS   How does Janet relax? What's the problem?

FEELINGS   How do you think Janet feels about two more hours of work?

AND YOU?   How do you relax?

SOUND BITES

Chan and his friend Janet go to Himmel Park.

Before You Listen In small groups talk about the words on the map.
What do you usually do at an art museum? at a science museum?
at a zoo? at a picnic? at a theater? at a concert? at a baseball field?

While You Listen Draw a line where Chan goes. Then draw a line
where Janet goes. Use different-colored pens or pencils.

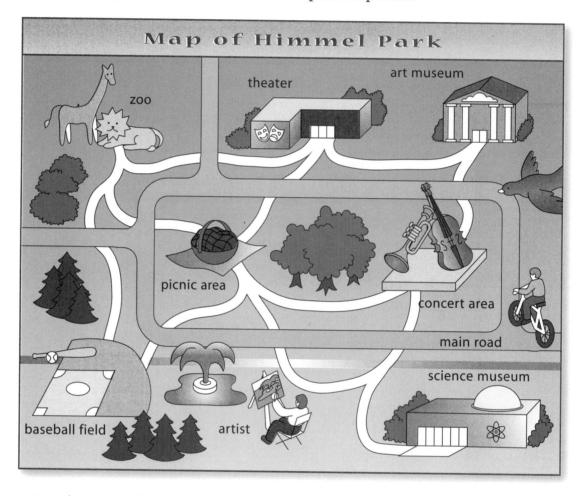

Map of Himmel Park

zoo

theater

art museum

picnic area

concert area

main road

science museum

baseball field

artist

After You Listen In small groups talk about how Janet and Chan relax.
Ask, "What do they do that's the same? What do they do that's different?"

Your Turn

Draw a map of a park or a shopping center in your city.
Plan your day there. Draw a line showing the places you want to visit.
Share your plan with a partner or a small group.

SPOTLIGHT ON SIMPLE PRESENT

Statements

I / You / We / They   **play** soccer.

visit the zoo.

listen to music.

go shopping.

Janet **goes** to the park.

Chan **plays** soccer.

Add **-s** to the verb with *he*, *she*, and *it*.

Negative Statements

I / You / We / They **do not (don't)**   **work** on Sunday.

eat in restaurants.

play baseball.

see plays.

She **does not (doesn't) like** shopping.

He **does not (doesn't) watch** TV.

doesn't = does not   *don't = do not*

Exercise 1: Gloria and Marta are sisters. Antonio is their brother. Here are their Saturday schedules—lists of their activities. Write sentences about their Saturdays. Use simple present.

Antonio		Gloria and Marta	
9:00–12:00	play soccer	10:00–1:00	go shopping
12:00–3:00	go on a picnic	1:00–2:00	eat lunch
3:00–5:00	go to a rock concert	2:00–5:00	go to the movies

1. Antonio ___plays soccer from 9:00 to 12:00___.

2. Antonio _____.

3. He _____.

4. He doesn't _____.

5. Gloria and Marta _____.

6. They _____.

7. They don't _____.

In Your Experience

Make a schedule of your Saturday or Sunday activities.
Tell a partner three things about your schedule.

In small groups talk about the words below.

relax   leisure   schedule   café

Person to Person

Listen to these conversations about leisure activities.
With a partner finish the last conversation.
Then practice the conversations with your partner.

GLORIA: What's the schedule for the day?

MARTA: Same as always. First we shop. Then we eat.

GLORIA: Sounds good! I *love* that café on First Avenue.
Let's go there for lunch.

CHAN: You work too hard. You need to relax.

GARY: I know. Man, I work 60 hours a week!

CHAN: We play soccer every day. You can play too.

GRACE: Janet has so much fun on the weekends.

ANTONIO: What does she do?

GRACE: She visits the park, she sees plays,
and she listens to concerts.

JOHN: Let's have some fun tonight. What do you
want to do?

ALEX: I don't know. I don't like sports or music,
and I don't watch TV.

JOHN: _____

ALEX: _____

In small groups talk about the words below.

recreation   performance   fee   supplies   uniform   nature   techniques

READING FOR REAL

Chan and Janet want to take recreation classes.
Here is the information they read about
programs in their community.

CITY RECREATION PROGRAMS

FOR ALL AGES

Mexican Folk Dance
Classes in dances from different
states. Performances given.
• Sat. 2:00–2:50 P.M.
• Adults
• Fee: $14 for 8 weeks

Drawing
Students will draw nature and people.
Dress in old clothes. Fee includes supplies.
• Wed. 4:30–5:20 P.M.
• 8 yrs. – Adult
• Fee: $31 for 8 weeks

Judo
Self-defense techniques.
Uniform necessary.
• Tue. 7:00–7:50 P.M.
• 5 yrs. – Adults
• Fee: $14 for 8 weeks

Swimming Lessons
Instruction for all skill levels, especially
beginners. Loma Verde Pool.
• Tue. and Thu. 7:00-8:00 P.M.
• 16 yrs. and over
• Fee: $23 for 10 lessons

 Exercise 2: Use the information in the
schedule to answer these questions.

1. Which class is for adults only?
   a. Mexican Folk Dance
   b. Judo
   c. Swimming Lessons
   d. Drawing

2. Which class meets two times a week?
   a. Mexican Folk Dance
   b. Judo
   c. Swimming Lessons
   d. Drawing

3. Chan wants to take judo.
   What does he need?
   a. self-defense
   b. old clothes
   c. a uniform

4. Which class costs the most?
   a. Mexican Folk Dance
   b. Judo
   c. Swimming Lessons
   d. Drawing

5. Can beginners take swimming lessons?
   a. yes
   b. no
   c. not sure

Talk About It

Why do people take recreation classes?
In which classes can you exercise?
Which class do you like?

In small groups talk about the words below.

stress   nervous   boss   relaxation techniques

CULTURE CORNER

Read about a big problem for working people
in the United States.

Working in the United States

Most people in the United States are busy, busy, busy. Employers want people to work hard and fast. Most people work 40 hours a week. Some people work 50 or 60 hours—or more! They don't have time to relax. Sometimes they get job stress. Job stress is a very real problem.

Exercise 3: Do you have job stress? Here are seven questions to answer. Write *Y* (yes) or *N* (no) in the blanks.

1. Do you often feel sad? _____

2. Do you often feel nervous? _____

3. Do you have trouble sleeping? _____

4. Do you feel angry about your job? _____

5. Is it difficult to get up in the morning to go to work? _____

6. Do you want to change jobs? _____

7. Are you angry with your boss? _____

Did you answer *yes* to most of the questions? Maybe you have job stress. Here are three things to do about your problems:

1. Talk to your boss.
2. Talk to someone at work.

3. Get a new job.

Exercise 4: Here are five ways to fight stress. Check (✔) if you do this now.

1. Exercise regularly. _____

2. Eat good food. _____

3. Take part in relaxing activities. _____

4. Learn relaxation techniques. _____

5. Get enough sleep. _____

Your Turn

Now ask a partner the seven job-stress questions.
Does your partner have job stress? Ask how your partner fights stress.

Talk about the pictures with a partner.

Ask each other the questions below.

Share your answers with another pair or the class.

Chan talks to his friend Paul about his vacation plans.

FACTS	What are Chan's trip plans? What's the problem?
FEELINGS	Paul is surprised by Chan's plans. Why?
AND YOU?	Some people never relax. Do you know any?

SOUND BITES

Chan is telling Paul about his trip schedule.

While You Listen Make a schedule for Chan's trip.

SATURDAY		SUNDAY	
Activity	Time	Activity	Time
set up camp	10:00–10:30		

After You Listen Make a more relaxing one-week schedule for Chan.

SPOTLIGHT ON VERB + INFINITIVE

	Verb	Infinitive	
Paul	**wants**	**to play**	the guitar.
We	**plan**	**to go**	dancing.
They	**like**	**to go**	to the park.

Exercise 5: Donna wrote a letter to her grandmother.
Complete the letter with *plan*, *want*, or *like*, and the words below.
Then copy the letter in your notebook.

to swim	to play the guitar	to go dancing
to run in the park	to go to the beach	to see a play

Dear Grandma,

I love my new home in San Diego, California.

There are lots of things to do. (1) _I like to go to the beach._
_____.

My friends and I (2)_____
_____.

We also (3) _____
_____.

My girlfriend (4) _____
_____too.

She (5)_____
_____.

Next weekend, we (6)_____

Love,

Donna

Person to Person

Listen to the conversation. Practice it with a partner.
Then change it to be true for you.

GLORIA: What are your plans for the weekend?

MARTA: I plan to see a play, and I want you to come too.

GLORIA: Sure! How much are tickets?

SPOTLIGHT ON ADVERBS OF FREQUENCY

I **always** watch TV on the weekends.

We **usually** play soccer.

You **often** go to museums.

She **sometimes** listens to music.

Paul **hardly ever** sees a movie.

Grace **never** plays the piano.

0%   20%   40%   60%   80%   100%

Exercise 6: Answer these questions about yourself.
Use the words in the chart. For example, write, "I sometimes watch TV."

1. Do you ever watch TV? _____

2. Do you ever go to the park? _____

3. Do you ever listen to music? _____

4. Do you ever go dancing? _____

5. Do you ever draw or paint? _____

6. Do you ever play the guitar? _____

7. Do you ever go to concerts? _____

8. Do you ever visit museums? _____

In Your Experience

Now think about your best friend, husband, wife, brother, or sister.
Talk to a partner, who will ask questions about the activities
that person likes to do. Here's an example.

YOU: I'm thinking about my friend Alina.

YOUR PARTNER: Does she ever watch TV?

In small groups talk about the words below.

electronics   VCR   CD player   camcorder

GET GRAPHIC

This bar graph tells about electronic products in the United States.
Bar graphs give information using words, numbers, and bars.

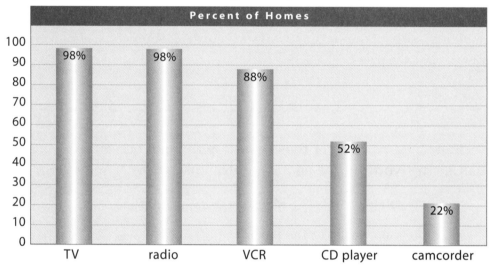

Percent of Homes

TV	98%
radio	98%
VCR	88%
CD player	52%
camcorder	22%

Kinds of Electronic Products in U.S. Homes in 1998

Exercise 7: Study the graph. Then answer the questions.

1. Which two products are found most often in homes in the United States?

   a. radios   b. TVs   c. camcorders

2. Write the percentage of homes with

   a. TVs _____   b. VCRs _____   c. CD players _____

3. Which product is not found very often in homes in the United States?

   a. radio   b. CD player   c. camcorder

In Your Experience

Divide into groups of eight. Take a survey on this question:
What electronic products do you have in your home?
Your teacher will help you make a bar graph of this information.

In small groups talk about the words below.

free   educational   violent

ISSUES AND ANSWERS

Janet and her friends are talking about television.
Some friends like TV, or are *for* it (*pro*).
Others don't like it, or are *against* it (*con*).
Read what they say about television.

PRO (FOR TV)	CON (AGAINST TV)
TV is relaxing.	TV is boring.
You learn new words from TV.	TV is too violent for children.
You learn about the news on TV.	TV has too many commercials.
Movies are free on TV.	People don't get enough exercise because they watch TV.
Children can practice reading on educational TV.	People don't read because they watch TV.

Your Turn

With a partner talk about the pros and cons of TV.
Write one sentence for TV and one sentence against it.
Then one partner writes your pro and con sentences on the chalkboard.
The other reads your two sentences to the class.
After all pairs do this, make a class poster of TV pros and cons.

WRAP-UP

With a partner complete the T-chart below. A T-chart helps you think
and write. In a T-chart, you write ideas on both sides of the T.
Write your ideas for fun things to do on the left side.
Write your partner's ideas for fun things to do on the right side.

MY IDEAS FOR FUN THINGS TO DO	MY PARTNER'S IDEAS FOR FUN THINGS TO DO
go to the park	watch TV

Now check the things you both like to do. Tell the class about those things.

Think About Learning

In this unit you learned a variety of skills and language structures.
Look at the items in the list below and check how easy or difficult
each item was for you. At the bottom write one other thing you learned.

SKILLS / STRUCTURES	Page	easy ☺	so-so ☺	difficult ☹
Talk about people's problems	13			
Listen to map directions	14			
Understand schedules	15			
Read a bar graph	22			
Present pros and cons of an issue	21			
Use a T-chart and present ideas	23			
Use the simple present tense	15			
Use verb + infinitive	20			
Use adverbs of frequency	21			

PROBLEM SOLVING
IN THE NEIGHBORHOOD

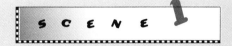

Talk about the pictures with a partner.
Ask each other the questions below.
Share your answers with another pair or the class.

FACTS   What's the problem? How did the neighbors solve their problem?

FEELINGS   How does the kitten feel? How does Kathy feel about the kitten?

AND YOU?   Did you ever have a problem like this in your neighborhood?
How did you solve the problem?

Now write or tell the story in your own words.

VOCABULARY PROMPTS

With a partner or small group talk about the words below.

Crime Stoppers   report   Neighborhood Watch   solve

SOUND BITES

Find out about a good neighborhood and about a problem.

Before You Listen Look at the pictures and read the questions below.

While You Listen Answer the questions below.

1. Are there trees and street lights
   in Samira's neighborhood?
   How does she feel about the lights?

   _____

   _____

2. What is the problem? Does the
   Crime Stoppers officer ask
   the caller's name?

   _____

   _____

3. What is a Neighborhood Watch meeting?
   What problem does Kathy want to solve?

   _____

   _____

After You Listen Talk about your answers with a partner or a small group.

In Your Experience

Write three sentences describing your neighborhood.
Share your sentences with the class.

Present Singular

There is a kitten on the roof.

Is there a kitten on the roof?

Yes, **there is**.

No, **there is not**.

No, **there isn't**.

No, **there's not**.

Present Plural

There are many students in the class.

Are there many students in the class?

Yes, **there are**. No, **there are not**.

No, **there aren't**.

Past Singular

There was a kitten on the roof (an hour ago).

Was there a kitten on the roof?

Yes, **there was**.

No, **there was not**.

No, **there wasn't**.

Past Plural

There were many students in the class.

Were there many students in the class?

Yes, **there were**.

No, **there weren't**.

Exercise 1: Write the missing words for the story on the lines below. Use the words in the list.

neighborhood   trash   trees   lights   playground

Maria's new neighborhood is beautiful. There are tall

(1) _____. There are also (2) _____

to help her see the street at night. There is a (3) _____

for children. There is no (4) _____ in the street.

Maria likes her (5) _____.

Your Turn

Your friend moves to a new neighborhood. In your notebook write three questions to ask about the new neighborhood. For example, ask, "Are there many street lights?"

In Your Experience

In a group ask each other one question about your neighborhood now (where you live now) and one question about your old neighborhood (where you lived before—in your native country or in the United States). For example, ask, "Is there a hospital in your neighborhood? Was there a hospital in your old neighborhood?"

Person to Person

Listen to these conversations. With a partner finish the last conversation. Use *there is* or *there are* if possible. Then practice all the conversations with your partner.

911 OPERATOR: Hello, 911.

CALLER: Hello, I think there's someone in my house. There were some noises downstairs a few minutes ago. Can you send someone quickly?

911 OPERATOR: What's your address?

CALLER: 682 Forest Street.

MARIA: Mrs. Lee, can you please take care of my dog for a few days?

MRS. LEE: Sure, I'll watch your dog. I'm always home.

MARIA: Great! There are three cans of dog food on the back stairs. Thanks a lot, Mrs. Lee.

MOTHER: Careful! There's a lot of traffic on this street!

CHILD: Mom, I'm always careful.

MOTHER: Well, some drivers aren't careful!

BOB: Darn it, there's too much crime in this neighborhood!

SECURITY GUARD: Now what happened?

BOB: _____

_____

_____

_____

VOCABULARY PROMPTS

In small groups talk about these words. If you need help, ask your teacher.

14-story   steel   tank   water district   customer

READING FOR REAL

There's a giant 14-story water tank in the Grossmont neighborhood of San Diego, California. It is made out of special brown steel and has 3.6 million gallons of water inside.

Source: Helix Water District.

The problem is that some people think the tank is very ugly. They don't like the way it looks in their neighborhood, so they want to change it. They want the Water District to paint it blue. These neighbors asked for a public meeting about the problem. Painting would cost $430,000.

At the meeting in August 1997, there were 350 people from Grossmont. Sixty-five of them spoke for or against painting the big brown tank. Finally, there were many phone calls and letters from neighborhood water customers to the Water District. Don't paint it, said 4,064 people. Paint it, said 105 other people. So the tall tank is still brown.

Exercise 2: Use the information above to answer these questions.

1. How tall is the water tank? _____

2. What do some people think about the tank? _____

3. How much would it cost to paint the tank? _____

4. Do you think meetings are a good way to change things? Why or why not?

_____

_____

Your Turn

Are there things you want to change in your school or classroom?
What are they? Talk in small groups. Then write a list on the chalkboard.
What can you do next?

In small groups talk about the words below.

interview   protect   property   advice   report

CULTURE CORNER

Read the story and interview with Cass Brown, a security guard.

In the United States, there are many jobs for security guards at stores, offices, hospitals, apartment buildings, and hotels. At these places, security guards protect people and property. They are not police officers, but they call the police. Cass Brown is a security guard. He walks around and checks 300 condominiums every afternoon. He writes a report every night.

Cecelia Ryan is one of the authors of this book.

CECELIA: Cass, what do you like about your job?

CASS: Well, I like the work hours here. My hours are 4:00 P.M. to 10:00 P.M., Monday through Friday. I take care of my daughter in the mornings. That's important for me.

CECELIA: What do you think makes a good neighborhood?

CASS: In a good neighborhood, people work together. They tell me or call the police if they see a crime.

CECELIA: How are things going in this neighborhood?

CASS: They're going pretty well, but there are problems with some kids.

CECELIA: What do you tell parents?

CASS: I want parents to come outside and see what their kids are doing. I also want parents to report problems.

CECELIA: Thanks for the information, Cass.

Your Turn

What do you think Cass writes in his reports?
In your notebook write three sentences that a security guard can write about an apartment building. For example, write, "There's a light out in the garage at 4359 Anthony Street, Apartment 15."

Talk about the pictures with a partner. Ask each other the questions below. Share your answers with another pair or the class.

Cha-Soon and Yung are Margarita's friends. They went to see her new house.

Hi! What did you bring me, Yung?

Congratulations on your new house, Margarita.

We brought you laundry soap for good luck. It's a Korean custom. Your money is going to grow like soap bubbles.

Thank you!

DETERGENT

FACTS What does Yung give Margarita? What's the problem?

FEELINGS How does Margarita feel at first? How does she feel later?

AND YOU? Do friends and family bring presents to new homeowners in your native country? What do they bring?

VOCABULARY PROMPTS

In small groups talk about the words below.

bought   paid   saved   down payment   mortgage

SOUND BITES

Before You Listen In a small group talk about ways to get money for a new house. Make a group list on a sheet of paper.

While You Listen Look at your list. Put a check next to the ideas that are the same as Margarita's.

After You Listen Check your list with another group's list. Add their ideas to your list. Share the new lists with the class.

SPOTLIGHT ON SIMPLE PAST OF REGULAR AND IRREGULAR VERBS

Use the simple past to talk about an activity completed in the past.

Many simple past verbs end in -ed, but many others have an iregular past form.

Here are some examples:

Regular		Irregular	
Simple Form	**Simple Past**	**Simple Form**	**Simple Past**
ask	asked	buy	bought
call	called	find	found
cook	cooked	get	got
finish	finished	go	went
play	played	say	said
stay	stayed	take	took
talk	talked	write	wrote

Exercise 3: Read about Cha-Soon's talk with Margarita.

Write the simple past form of one of the verbs above on the lines below.

Yesterday Cha-Soon (1) _____*went*_____ to see Margarita's new house.

Margarita (2) _____ to Cha-Soon for a long time. Margarita

(3) _____ that she (4) _____ the house for $120,000.

She (5) _____ it for sale in a nice neighborhood.

It (6) _____ five years for her family to save $20,000.

They (7) _____ the bank for a $100,000 loan.

Person to Person

Listen to the conversations. Practice them with a partner.
Then change them to be true for you.

CHA-SOON: I went to see Margarita's new house!

KATHY: I bet you liked it.

CHA-SOON: Yes, now I'm saving money to buy a house too.

CHA-SOON: I saved some money today!

YOUNG: That's great! How?

CHA SOON: I took my lunch to work.

SPOTLIGHT ON PREPOSITIONS OF LOCATION

The words *inside*, *outside*, *beside*, *between*, and *behind* tell where something or somebody is.

outside

inside

beside

between

behind

Exercise 4: Complete the sentences with the words above.
Check your work with a partner.

1. Kathy's kitten is walking _____ a man's feet.

2. Kathy's kitten doesn't like to stay _____.

3. There's a kitten _____ the trash can.

4. Kathy's kitten is walking _____ a woman.

5. The kitten is safe _____ the house.

Your Turn

In your notebook make sentences with the words below.
For example, write, "There is a security guard between the cars."

There is	a young man	beside		street light
There are	kittens	outside	the	door
	children	between		cars
	trash cans	behind	the	apartment

Talk about the words with a partner or in a small group.
If you need help, ask your teacher.

patrol   checklist   exterior   elevators   lobby   shift

GET GRAPHIC

This is the patrol checklist for security guards in a hotel. A different guard patrols the hotel in each shift. Morning shift is 7:00 A.M. to 3:30 P.M. Afternoon shift is 3:30 P.M. to 11:00 P.M. Night shift is 11:00 P.M. to 7:00 A.M. Each guard writes the patrol time and any problems on the chart.

Read the chart. Look at the time by each place. Some lines have no words because the night-shift guard is still checking. There was a problem with the exterior lights in the morning.

	MORNING SHIFT	AFTERNOON SHIFT	NIGHT SHIFT
STAIRWAY	7:10	3:08	10:19
ELEVATOR	7:31	3:29	11:12
BATHROOMS	9:10	4:14	12:16
EXTERIOR LIGHTS	south corner out	OK 5:35	1:18
GARAGE	12:00	6:00	1:30
PARKING LOT	1:05	6:32	7:10
FRONT DOOR	2:15	7:18	
REAR DOOR	2:19	7:22	
SWIMMING POOL	2:36	8:58	

Exercise 5: Answer these questions in your notebook.
Then share your answers with a partner.

1. How many times a day are the elevators checked?

2. What was wrong with the south corner exterior light this morning? How do you know?

3. What is the night-shift guard going to check?

Your Turn

Make a list of five places a security guard can check at your school.
Talk about your answers in a small group. Choose the five best answers.
Then present them to the class.

Talk about the words below with a partner or a small group.

skills   firecrackers

ISSUES AND ANSWERS

Read the letters below. Talk about them with a partner.
Write Anita's answer in your notebook.

Ask ABDUL and ANITA

DEAR ABDUL,

In my building there's a very good security guard. He told me there is a security guard job open now. I like to walk, and I have good eyes. I'm a careful person. Do you need good English to be a guard?

NEEDS A JOB

DEAR NEEDS A JOB,

To be a security guard, you need good English skills. Guards listen to information and ask and answer questions. They also read checklists and write daily reports. Good luck!

ABDUL

DEAR ANITA,

I saw a boy playing with firecrackers behind my apartment. I called the security guard. She came and told the boy to stop. Did I do the right thing?

MARIA

DEAR GOOD NEIGHBOR,

_____
_____
_____
_____
_____

ANITA

WRAP-UP

The chart below is a T-chart. It can help you organize your ideas about a security guard's job. With a partner complete the chart. Write good things (advantages) about being a security guard on the left side. Write bad things (disadvantages) on the right.

SECURITY GUARDS	
Advantages	**Disadvantages**
They stop crimes.	They can get hurt.

In a group of three, talk about the advantages and disadvantages of a security guard's job. Write three sentences for each side. Then each person should present one idea from each side of the chart to the class.

Think About Learning

In this unit you learned a variety of skills and language structures. Look at the items in the list below and check how easy or difficult each item was for you. At the bottom write one other thing you learned.

SKILLS / STRUCTURES	Page	easy ☺	so-so ☺	difficult ☹
Listen to safety ideas	26			
Speak about neighborhood life	28			
Solve a public problem	29			
Learn about a job as a guard	30			
Read and write a report	34			
Use *there is/there are/there was/there were*	27			
Use irregular past	32			
Use prepositions of location	33			
Complete a T-chart	36			

UNIT 4 SUCCESSFUL AMERICANS

Talk about the pictures in a small group.
Ask each other the questions below.
Share your answers with the rest of the class.

FACTS   What do you see in the classroom? What is on the paper?
Who is speaking to the teacher?
What is Carmen's job in the group?

FEELINGS   Why does the group feel good?

AND YOU?   Do you like to work in groups or alone? Why?

SOUND BITES

Listen to stories of six successful Americans.

Before You Listen With a partner read the paragraph below.
Then talk about the places. Ask where the countries are.

To be *successful* means to do something well. These six people
became successful at their jobs. They were all *immigrants* to the
United States—they moved here from other places.

China   Puerto Rico   Scotland   Cuba   Czechoslovakia

While You Listen In the chart write the native countries of these
people and the dates they moved to the United States.
Use the names in the list above.

	SUCCESSFUL AMERICAN	Name of Native Country	Date Moved to the United States
	1. Martina Navratilova	Czechoslovakia	1975
	2. An Wang		
	3. Alexander Graham Bell		
	4. Roberto Clemente		
	5. Gloria Estefan		
	6. Madeleine Albright		

After You Listen Check your answers with a partner.

Your Turn

With your partner ask and answer questions about the people listed above.

YOU: Do you know anything about Martina Navratilova?

YOUR PARTNER: Yes, I do. She is from Czechoslovakia. She moved to
                the United States in 1975, and she plays tennis.

I/You/He/She/We/They   **worked** in Mexico.

I/You/He/She/We/They   **moved** to the United States in 1995.

Regular simple past verbs end in *-ed.*

Use simple past to talk about an action completed in the past.

Spelling Rules

Add **-d** or **-ed** to most verbs (**learn + -ed = learned**   **move + -d = moved**)

Drop the **-y** and add **-ied** to verbs ending in a consonant + **y,** (**study + ed = studied**)

Add **-ed** to verbs ending in a vowel + **y** (**play + ed = played**)

Pronunciation Rules

The past forms are pronounced in three different ways:

1. The **-ed** is pronounced /**t**/ when the verb ends in the sounds
   of the consonants **ch, sh, f, k, p, s, x** (**worked, watched, helped**).

2. The **-ed** is pronounced /**id**/ when the verb ends in the sounds
   of the consonants **d** or **t** (**started, invented, decided**).

3. The **-ed** is pronounced /**d**/ for all other sounds (**moved, played, learned**).

Exercise 1: Fill in the blanks with the simple past of these words.

start   move   play   learn

We (1) ___*learned*___ about famous women immigrants today.

Gloria Estefan is a famous singer. She (2) _____ to the

United States from Cuba in 1959. Martina Navratilova (3) _____

to the United States from Czechoslovakia in 1975. At a young age, she

(4) _____ tennis very well. Madeleine Albright is from

Czechoslovakia too. She (5) _____ to the United States in 1948.

As U.S. secretary of state under President Clinton, she is an important person

in Washington, D.C. She (6) _____ her job there in 1997.

 In Your Experience

In your notebook make two sentences about your life.

Use these words: *moved, started, the United States,* and *school.*

Share the sentences with your partner.

Check your partner's pronunciation of the *-ed* verbs.

Person to Person

Listen to the conversations. With a partner, finish the last
conversation with the simple past. Then practice the conversations.

CARMEN: Why is Madeleine Albright famous?

TEACHER She is the first woman to be the secretary
of state for the United States. She started
that job in 1997.

CARMEN: I see. Thanks.

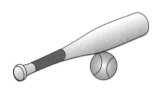

WILLIAM: Do you know anything about Roberto
Clemente?

TAMARA: He played baseball very well, and he helped
many people.

WILLIAM: Wasn't he from Puerto Rico?

KIM: Isn't that woman on TV Oprah Winfrey?

TEACHER: Yes. Oprah was from a poor family, but she
was smart, and she worked hard. Now she is
one of the richest people in the United States.

KIM: That's interesting.

TAMARA: What do you know about
Alexander Graham Bell?

CARMEN: _____

_____

TAMARA: I didn't know that.

 Your Turn

With a partner, present one of the conversations to the class.

READING FOR REAL

Carmen, Kim, William, and Tamara read about the job experience of a successful American, Oprah Winfrey. Then they wrote a work history about her. Read the history in a small group.

 Exercise 2: Circle the correct answers.

WORK HISTORY—OPRAH WINFREY

Dates	Job Experience
1988 to Present	Producer and owner of Harpo Production Studio
1985 to Present	National talk-show host for The Oprah Winfrey Show
1985 to Present	Actress—movies and TV
1984 to 1985	Talk-show host for A.M. Chicago in Chicago, Illinois
1977 to 1983	Talk-show co-host in Baltimore, Maryland
1976 to 1977	TV news anchorperson and reporter in Baltimore, Maryland
1973 to 1976	TV news co-anchor in Nashville, Tennessee
1970 to 1973	Radio newscaster (part-time position) in Nashville, Tennessee

1. Oprah started to work in
   a. 1970.
   b. 1973.
   c. 1988.

2. She worked in
   a. Tennessee and Washington, D.C.
   b. Tennessee and Maryland only.
   c. Tennessee, Maryland, and Illinois.

3. In 1973, Oprah lived in
   a. Chicago.
   b. Nashville.
   c. Baltimore.

4. She worked at a radio station for
   a. one year.
   b. three years.
   c. twenty years.

5. The experience in her work history
   a. starts with her present jobs.
   b. starts with her most important job.
   c. starts with her first job.

 ### Talk About It

How many jobs does Oprah have now?
How many years did she work before she had her own show?
What kind of work did she do before she was a talk-show host?

  ### In Your Experience

Write your work history. Then share it with your group.

 # CULTURE CORNER

In small groups read about leading a group.

LEADING A GROUP

In many U.S. classrooms, students learn to work in groups or teams.
In many jobs in this country, people work in teams too.
The members on the team work together. Each member may have a
different job or role in the group. The leader's role is very important.
Here are three things the leader of a classroom needs to do.

1. The leader starts the group working.
2. The leader helps the other members understand the work.
3. The leader makes sure all the members are participating.

Exercise 3: Here are some questions and expressions to use
when you are the leader. In your group write the best word
to complete the question or expression.

do   help   begin   ready   think   understand

LEADER'S ROLE	LEADER SAYS
To start the group working	It's time to start. Are you (1) _____ ? Let's (2) _____ .
To help the other members	What's the problem? Do you (3) _____ ? Can I (4) _____ you?
To make sure all members are participating	Please share your ideas. What do you (5) _____ ? (6) _____ you agree?

  In Your Experience

In a group ask and answer these questions:

Do you like to be the leader? Why or why not?
Do you work in teams in your job?
How are teams different in a job and in school?

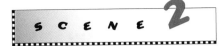

Talk about the pictures with a partner.
Ask each other the questions below.
Share your answers with another pair or the class.

Bill Gates was born in 1965. In 1975 he started a software company called Microsoft.

Did you say 1975? Did he start the company at age ten?

Oops, we made a mistake. Gates was born in 1955, not 1965.

FACTS What's the problem? What mistake did Kim make?

FEELINGS Do you think Kim and William are upset?

AND YOU? Do you ever make mistakes in class? How do you feel?

VOCABULARY PROMPTS

Before you listen, talk about these words in a small group.

Washington   Harvard University   software   achievement

SOUND BITES

While You Listen In your notebook, write answers to these questions about Bill Gates.

Where was Gates born? What university did he go to?
What did he develop for computers?

After You Listen Check your answers with a partner.

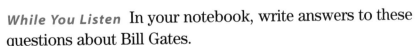

SPOTLIGHT ON SIMPLE PAST IN YES/NO QUESTIONS AND NEGATIVE STATEMENTS

| **Did** Bill Gates | **live** | in Ohio? | No, he **didn't**. |
| **Did** he | **work** | for IBM? | |

| **Did** | Sandra Cisneros | **write** | a play? | No, she **didn't**. |
| **Did** | she | **live** | in Washington? | |

did not = didn't

Exercise 4: Lisa's group wrote a report on Sandra Cisneros, a Mexican-American author. Cisneros was born in the city of Chicago, Illinois. She writes wonderful stories, novels, and poems. The class asked Lisa and Dave questions about the author. Complete the interview with simple past questions and negative statements.

Source: AP/Wide World Photos

WILLIAM: (1) *Cisneros / come* ___Did Cisneros come___ from a small family?

LISA: No, she (2) ___didn't___. She has six brothers.

TAMARA: (3) *she / write* _____ her novel *Woman Hollering Creek* first?

LISA: No, she (4) _____. *The House on Mango Street* was her first novel.

KIM: (5) *she / stay* _____ in Chicago, her hometown?

DAVE: No, she (6) _____. She now lives in San Antonio, Texas.

SPOTLIGHT ON PAST TIME EXPRESSIONS

Cisneros had an idea **three years ago**.

She wrote a book **last year**.

When did you **last** buy a book?

I bought one **yesterday**.

More Time Expressions

the day before yesterday   the night before last   last night/week/month

yesterday morning/afternoon/evening   a minute/an hour/a week/a month/ago

 Exercise 5: Look at the time line for Lisa's group report.

divided the work	read articles	wrote the report	practiced the presentation	presented the report
Sept. 30	Oct. 15	Oct. 22–25	Oct. 27	Oct. 29

 Exercise 6: Lisa's group worked for a month on the report.
Read her sentences and look at the time line above.
Complete her sentences with the time expressions below.

yesterday   two weeks ago   last month   last week   three days ago

1. Today is October 30. _____ Last month _____, we divided the work on our Sandra Cisneros project.

2. We presented the report to the class _____.

3. _____ we practiced our oral presentation.

4. We wrote the final report _____.

5. _____ we read articles about her.

  Person to Person

Listen to the conversation. Practice it with a partner.
Then change it to be true for you.

LISA: When did you start your report?

CARMEN: We started five weeks ago.

LISA: Wow! My group didn't start until last week.

GET GRAPHIC

Lisa's class made an *illustrated time line* of the
American leaders from their projects. The illustrated time
line shows the dates of achievements—important things
they did—and pictures of those achievements.

ACHIEVEMENTS OF FAMOUS AMERICANS		
Alexander Graham Bell invented the first telephone	1876	
Roberto Clemente was voted the Most Valuable Player in baseball	1966	
Bill Gates began Microsoft, Inc.	1975	
Oprah Winfrey started her TV show, *The Oprah Winfrey Show*	1985	
Sandra Cisneros won the PEN Center West Award for fiction	1992	
Madeleine Albright became U.S. secretary of state.	1997	

 Exercise 7: Choose the correct answer.

1. On this illustrated time line, the pictures represent
   a. the years.
   b. famous people's achievements.
   c. the sports.

2. The medal represents
   a. Bill Gates.
   b. Oprah Winfrey.
   c. Sandra Cisneros.

3. The earliest achievement was by
   a. Alexander Graham Bell.
   b. Oprah Winfrey.
   c. Madeleine Albright.

4. The most recent achievement was by
   a. Alexander Graham Bell.
   b. Oprah Winfrey.
   c. Madeleine Albright.

 Your Turn

In a small group look at the achievements of a
famous person from this unit. Make an illustrated time line.

In small groups talk about the words below.
These are words for possible *qualities* of leaders.

hard-working   positive   cooperative   responsible

intelligent   powerful

ISSUES AND ANSWERS

Lisa and Kim are talking about the qualities of a leader.

LISA: I think a leader needs to be very intelligent.

KIM: Leaders don't really need to be intelligent.
Many are just lucky. They are in the right place
at the right time.

LISA: Think about Madeleine Albright! She has to be
smart to work at the United Nations and become
U.S. secretary of state.

Exercise 8: In a small group talk about qualities of a leader.
Look at the words above. Ask and answer:
Which qualities do most leaders have?
Which qualities can help but are not necessary?
Give examples of the qualities of some leaders. Make a T-chart.
Share your chart with the class.

VERY IMPORTANT QUALITIES FOR LEADERS	LESS IMPORTANT QUALITIES FOR LEADERS

WRAP-UP

Read the story about Bill Gates.

Bill Gates was born in Seattle, Washington, in 1955. He was a good student. He entered Harvard University, but he didn't finish at Harvard. Instead, he started a company with a friend in 1975. They called their company Microsoft.

Gates did well. In 1985 the company made the Windows computer program for PCs—personal computers. His success was incredible. By 1986 Gates was one of the richest people in the United States, and he was only 30 years old!

Make an illustrated time line of Bill Gates's life and achievements in your notebook. Here's an example.

Bill Gates was born in 1955, in Seattle, Washington.

Write simple past questions about the story and your time line. Find a partner. Ask and answer questions. For example, ask, "Did Bill Gates start a company in 1975?"

Think About Learning

In this unit you learned a variety of skills and language structures. Look at the items in the list below and check how easy or difficult each item was for you. At the bottom write one other thing you learned.

SKILLS / STRUCTURES	Page	easy ☺	so-so 😐	difficult ☹
Talk about group work	42			
Learn about successful Americans	38			
Read a work history	41			
Understand a time line	46			
Read about qualities of a leader	47			
Use regular simple past	39			
Use simple past in yes/no questions and negative statements	44			
Use past time expressions	45			

SHAPE UP!

 S C E N E 1

Talk about the pictures with a partner.
Ask each other the questions below.
Share your answers with another pair or the class.

Henri and Mark are at work.

> Henri, you need to exercise. Have you thought about riding your bike to work?

> I can't. I sold it.

> How about going dancing with Anne?

> I can't. I don't date her anymore.

> Hey, we have two more hours of work!

> I'm taking a break. Our talk about exercise made me tired.

FACTS	What's the problem? What does Mark want Henri to do?
FEELINGS	How does Henri feel about Mark's plan? How does Henri really feel about exercise?
AND YOU?	What kind of exercise do you do?

VOCABULARY PROMPTS

Before you listen, talk about the words and pictures below in small groups.

Ways to Exercise

basketball   hiking   rollerblading   swimming

martial arts   aerobics   bicycling   jogging

SOUND BITES

A radio station is taking a survey to ask people about their exercise habits.

While You Listen Complete the chart on the five callers.

Caller	Age	Kind of Exercise	How Often
Caller 1	33		
Caller 2	48		
Caller 3	19		
Caller 4	25		
Caller 5	51		

After You Listen In small groups compare exercise plans for each person from the radio survey. Who exercises most? Who exercises least?

In Your Experience

Talk to a partner about exercise. Ask and answer these questions.

What exercise do you like best?

What exercise do you like least?

SPOTLIGHT ON DIRECT OBJECT PRONOUNS

Tina does aerobics. She does **them** every day.

Mark takes karate class. He takes **it** once a week.

Victor likes Marisa. He likes **her** very much.

Vera takes Angelo to skate. She takes **him** to the park.

Our karate teacher helps **us**. She helps **you** with kicks,
    and she helps **me** with form.

In the sentences above, the direct object answers the questions *who* or *what*.

Exercise 1: Study the pronouns chart below.

Subject Pronouns	I	you	he	she	it	we	they
Direct Object Pronouns	me	you	him	her	it	us	them

With the class look at the sentences at the top of the page.
Find all the subjects—nouns and pronouns. Then find all the direct
objects—nouns and pronouns.

Exercise 2: In your notebook complete the sentences below
with direct object pronouns.

People exercise for many reasons. Lynn exercises to lose weight.

She rides her bicycle. She rides (1) _____it_____ around the neighborhood.

Vera exercises for fun. She is teaching her little brother Angelo to skate.

She takes (2) _____ to the park on Sundays. Mark has problems

sleeping. Exercise helps (3) _____ to sleep better. Tina exercises

for her health. She takes aerobics classes at the YMCA. She takes

(4) _____ three days a week. Victor takes karate classes to relax.

He has his brown belt in karate. He earned (5) _____ last month.

Henri wants to get in shape. Now he has a conditioning machine.

He bought (6) _____ on sale. Doctors know that exercise

is important for us. They want (7) _____ to exercise 20 minutes

at least three times a week.

VOCABULARY PROMPTS

In small groups talk about the words below.

lose weight   heart attack   give up

Person to Person

Listen to these conversations about exercise. With a partner finish the last conversation. Then practice the conversations with a partner.

HENRI: I want to lose weight.

MARK: Well, you can't do that without hard work. Try to eat less and exercise more.

HENRI: I try to exercise, but then I give up.

TINA: I'm worried. My father has heart problems. Maybe I have them too.

LYNN: Do you exercise?

TINA: Not very much.

ANGELO: I want to exercise, but I'm too tired at the end of the day. I only want to watch TV.

VERA: You can do a few exercises every day.

ANGELO: I guess I can. Maybe I can do them before work.

LAURA: I want to exercise, but I'm afraid. What if I have a heart attack?

VICTOR: Check with your doctor before you exercise. You can call for an appointment.

LAURA: _____

                _____

In small groups talk about the words below.

heart disease   risk factors   cholesterol   stress   survey

READING FOR REAL

Take this survey on risk factors for heart disease.
Do you have two or more risk factors?
If you do, you need to learn to control them.

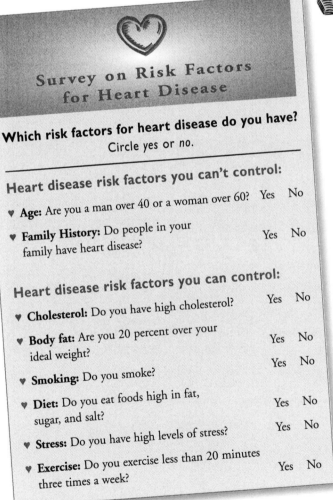

Survey on Risk Factors for Heart Disease

Which risk factors for heart disease do you have?
Circle yes or no.

Heart disease risk factors you can't control:

♥ **Age:** Are you a man over 40 or a woman over 60?   Yes   No

♥ **Family History:** Do people in your family have heart disease?   Yes   No

Heart disease risk factors you can control:

♥ **Cholesterol:** Do you have high cholesterol?   Yes   No

♥ **Body fat:** Are you 20 percent over your ideal weight?   Yes   No

♥ **Smoking:** Do you smoke?   Yes   No

♥ **Diet:** Do you eat foods high in fat, sugar, and salt?   Yes   No

♥ **Stress:** Do you have high levels of stress?   Yes   No

♥ **Exercise:** Do you exercise less than 20 minutes three times a week?   Yes   No

Exercise 2: Circle the correct answers to these questions about the survey.

1. Which risk factor *can't* you control?
   a. age
   b. cholesterol
   c. smoking

2. Which risk factor *can* you control?
   a. age
   b. family history
   c. exercise

3. Which group generally has heart disease at a younger age?
   a. men
   b. women

4. People 10 percent over their ideal weight are
   a. at risk for heart disease.
   b. not at risk for heart disease.

5. How much should you exercise per week?
   a. at least 30 minutes five times a week
   b. at least 20 minutes three times a week

Talk About It

What risks do you have for heart disease?
Which risk is difficult for you to control?

VOCABULARY PROMPTS

In small groups talk about the words below.

fad diet   nutrients   go on a diet   protein   side effect   liquid

CULTURE CORNER

Read the information about diets in the United States.

Losing weight is important to many people in the United States. People don't want to weigh too much. They see thin models in magazines and on TV. They want to look thin too.

For this reason people in the United States often go on diets. They make a plan to lose weight. Sometimes they choose fad diets. These diets are not healthy. People on them sometimes lose weight, but they usually gain it back quickly. And fad diets can cause health problems too.

Here are four kinds of fad diets people in the United States go on:

water only   **pills and medications**
mostly protein   **liquid diet**

Here are some of the possible problems with fad diets:
You need a doctor's supervision.
You may not get the nutrients you need.
The diets often do not work for long.
They can cause negative side effects.

There are safer ways to lose weight:
Don't eat fatty foods. Exercise regularly.
Eat fruits and vegetables.
Lose weight slowly.

Your Turn

Write two questions about diets in the United States.
Ask your partner the questions.

In Your Experience

In a group ask these questions.

Have you tried to lose weight? What diet works for you?
Is it a fad diet? Do people go on diets in your native country?

SCENE 2

Talk about the pictures with a partner.
Ask each other the questions below.
Share your answers with another pair or the class.

I am so sick. I hurt all over! I can't work today. I'm going to call in sick.

Hello. I'm sick. I'm not going to come in to work today.

STARK, JONES COMPANY

Yes? Who is speaking? Who is this? Oh, no, . . . he hung up!

FACTS   What is Mark's problem? What is he doing?

FEELINGS   How does the woman on the phone feel? Why?

AND YOU?   Do you call someone at work if you are sick? Explain.

SOUND BITES

Before You Listen What reasons do people give for not coming to work? In a small group talk about these reasons. Write your answers in your notebook.

While You Listen Listen to the phone calls about missing work. Write the reason and the number of days off work for each caller.

PERSON	REASON	NUMBER OF DAYS ABSENT
Henri		
Vera		
Victor		

After You Listen Compare your reasons with the reasons on the tape. Which reasons are the same? Which reasons are different?

I **am (I'm) going to take** karate.

Vera **is (Vera's) going to exercise** tomorrow.

You **are (You're) going to jog** every day.

We **are (We're) going to lose** weight.

Laura and Angelo **are going to eat** well.

I **am (I'm not) going to take** aerobics.

She **is (She's) not going to exercise** today.

You **are (You're) not going to jog** at night.

We **are (We're) not going to eat** too much.

They **are (They're) not going to eat** junk food.

Use *going to* + verb to talk about things in the near future.

Exercise 3: What healthy actions are you going to take next week? Write three sentences using *going to* in the chart below. You can write about food, exercise, or sleep. For example, write, "I'm going to drink six glasses of water every day." Next find a partner. Tell each other your sentences. Write your partner's sentences in the next column. Then write actions you and your partner share.

YOUR ACTIONS	YOUR PARTNER'S ACTIONS	ANSWERS YOU AND YOUR PARTNER SHARE

Person to Person

Listen to the conversation. Practice it with a partner.
Then change it to be true for you.

VICTOR: I'm not going to go to work tomorrow.

LYNN: Oh, really? Why not?

VICTOR: I have a bad cold and a headache.

Count Nouns

How **many hours** of sleep do you get?

I sleep **a few hours** every night.
I sleep **many hours** every night.

How **many days** of vacation does Henri take?
Henri takes **a few days** of vacation.

Noncount Nouns

How **much exercise** does Vera get?

She gets **a little** exercise.
She gets **a lot of** exercise.

How **much time** do Mark and Lynn have?
They have **a little** time.

Count nouns are separate things: *hours, girls, desks, problems*.
It is easy to count them.
Use *many* and *a few* with count nouns.
Noncount nouns are wholes: *exercise, sleep, water, sugar*.
It is *not* easy to count or separate them.
Use *much* or *a lot of* and *a little* with noncount nouns.

Exercise 4: Complete the sentences.
Use *many, much, a lot of, a few,* or *a little.*

DOCTOR: How (1) _____ exercise do you get?

LYNN: I get (2) _____ exercise. I walk two times a week.

DOCTOR: How (3) _____ hours of sleep do you get?

LYNN: I get (4) _____ hours of sleep.
Usually I get five or six hours.

DOCTOR: How (5) _____ sick days do you take each year?

LYNN: I take (6) _____ sick days each year.
Last year I took three.

DOCTOR: Do you have (7) _____ time to relax?

LYNN: I have (8) _____ time to relax.
I read for an hour every day.

In Your Experience

Find a partner. Ask the doctor's questions.

In small groups talk about the words below.

illness   personal business   death

GET GRAPHIC

Read the information and study the graph below.

A company listed reasons why workers missed work.
This pie graph shows percentages of reasons.
Pie graphs give information using
a circle, words, and numbers.

REASONS FOR MISSING WORK

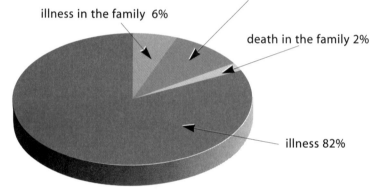

personal business 10%

illness in the family 6%

death in the family 2%

illness 82%

Exercise 5: First talk about the words on the graph with the class.
Then answer the questions about the graph.

1. On a pie graph all the percentages (%) added together equal

   a. 18%.   b. 82%.   c. 100%.

2. Write the percentage of absences due to

   a. illness _____

   b. personal business _____

   c. illness in the family _____

3. Circle the most common reason for absence from work.

   a. illness   b. personal business   c. death in the family

Your Turn

Ask other students why they miss work or school. Your teacher
will help you make a class pie graph of this information.

ISSUES AND ANSWERS

Read the letters below. If you don't know the meaning of a word, ask your teacher. Write an answer to "Up in Smoke."

Ask DOCTOR BROWNLEE

DEAR DR. BROWNLEE,

I have a problem. I can't go to sleep at night. I lie awake for hours. Finally, I sleep a little. I wake up early in the morning. I'm tired all day. I have problems at work because I'm sleepy. What can I do?

TOO TIRED

DEAR DR. BROWNLEE,

I have bad headaches about three times a week. I take aspirin, but my head still hurts. What can I do?

IT HURTS

DEAR DR. BROWNLEE,

I want to stop smoking. I know it's bad for my health. My wife really wants me to stop. She is afraid I'll have a heart attack. I have tried many times, but I can't stop. Do you have any ideas? I'm desperate.

UP IN SMOKE

DEAR TOO TIRED,

You may be feeling stress, or you may be depressed. See your doctor. Here are some other ideas to help you sleep better.
- Get regular exercise.
- Don't exercise during the two hours before bedtime.
- Don't drink coffee after 3:00 P.M.
- Sleep only at night. Don't take naps.
- Drink a glass of warm milk before bedtime.

DR. BROWNLEE

DEAR IT HURTS,

Do you get a headache after work? Maybe it's a tension headache. Do you have it on one side of the head? Maybe it's a migraine headache. There are different kinds of headaches. See a doctor and get a check-up. A doctor can find the problem.

DR. BROWNLEE

DEAR UP IN SMOKE,

_____
_____
_____
_____
_____
_____
_____

DR. BROWNLEE

 # WRAP-UP

Mark wants to sleep better. He is going to follow the doctor's suggestions.
A time line shows information according to when it happens.
This time line shows what Mark will do each day.

| 4:00–5:00 P.M. | 8:00–10:00 P.M. | 10:15 P.M. | 10:30 P.M. |
| swim | watch TV or read | drink a glass of warm milk | go to bed |

Write a paragraph about his personal time line.
Use *going to* in your writing.

Mark is going to swim from 4:00 to 5:00 P.M.

_____

_____

_____

 Think About Learning

In this unit you learned a variety of skills and language structures. Look at the items in the list below and check how easy or difficult each item was for you. At the bottom write one other thing you learned.

SKILLS / STRUCTURES	Page	easy ☺	so-so 😐	difficult ☹
Talk about people's problems	49			
Listen to conversations	52			
Understand a survey	53			
Read a pie graph	58			
Read about problems and solutions	59			
Use a time line	60			
Use direct object pronouns	51			
Use count and noncount nouns	58			
Use the future with *going to*	56			

UNIT 6   HOME, SWEET HOME

Talk about the pictures with a partner.
Ask each other the questions below.
Share your answers with another pair or with the class.

Hello. I'm Alex Costa, and this is my son. Hey, these apartments are great! How much is a two-bedroom?

Rent for a two-bedroom is $825 a month, plus a pet deposit. Do you have any pets?

Let's see . . . we have eight pets.

How many pets? Sorry. We really can't help you!

FACTS   What's the problem? What does Alex want?

FEELINGS   How does the manager feel about the pets?

AND YOU?   Do you rent an apartment? Do you have pets?
Was it difficult for you to get an apartment?

Before you listen, talk about the words below in small groups.

depressed   part-time job   security deposit

SOUND BITES

Listen to the conversation between Alex and his friend Dan.

While You Listen Alex has a problem with his apartment. Think about these questions: What is his problem? What is his solution? Take notes on the lines below.

Problem:

What's wrong with his apartment now?

_____

How many bedrooms does Alex want?

_____

Why doesn't he get a bigger place?

_____

Solution:

What is Alex going to do?

_____

_____

After You Listen In small groups talk about Alex's problem. Do you like his solution? What is another solution?

In Your Experience

In small groups talk about rent for apartments in your city or town. Look in the classified ads in your newspaper to find information. Ask and answer these questions.

Are apartments expensive in your neighborhood?
How much is a one-bedroom apartment?
How much is a two-bedroom apartment?
How much is a security deposit?

SPOTLIGHT ON *HOW MUCH* AND *HOW MANY*

How many   children do you have?

pets does Alex have?

bedrooms are there?

How much   money does he owe?

rent do you pay?

is the deposit?

Use *how many* before count nouns in questions.

Use *how much* before noncount nouns in questions.

Remember that *count nouns* are separate things.

It is easy to count them.

Remember that *noncount nouns* are whole things.

It is *not* easy to count or separate them.

VOCABULARY PROMPTS

In small groups talk about the words below.

accountant   bank account   account balance

Exercise 1: Read Alice's rental application.

RENTAL APPLICATION FORM

Alice Hunter	236 w. 7th St.	
Name	*Address*	
3 years	1 year	
Years at current address	*Years at previous address*	
998-2038	$980	accountant
Bank account number	*Account balance*	*Occupation*
Roget's, Inc.	5 months	2
Employer	*Years at job*	*Number of children*

Exercise 2: Circle the correct word, *many* or *much*. Then use Alice's application to answer the questions in your notebook.

1. How (*many* / *much*) years was Alice at her previous address?
   She was at her previous address 1 year.

2. How (*many* / *much*) money does she have in the bank?

3. How (*many* / *much*) months was Alice at her job?

4. How (*many* / *much*) children does she have?

5. How (*many* / *much*) jobs does she have?

Person to Person

If you rent an apartment, you will probably need to pay a *security deposit*. A security deposit is an extra payment to an apartment manager to pay for any possible damage to the apartment. The deposit is often one month's rent.

If you take good care of your apartment, the manager will return your deposit money when you move out. Many managers ask for a higher security deposit if you have pets.

Listen to these conversations about housing. With a partner finish the last conversation. Then practice the conversations with a partner.

LISA: How much is the security deposit?

MANAGER: It's $650.

LISA: Hmm, that's a lot of money.

DAN: How many pets do you have?

ALEX: We have 17 pets—2 dogs and 15 white mice.

DAN: You're kidding! How much is the security deposit for your apartment?

JULIE: What's the next question on our rental application?

HUSBAND: It's "How much money do you have in your bank account?"

JULIE: Let me see. We have about $1000.

RICK: I found a great apartment.

CHRIS: How many bedrooms does it have?

RICK: _____

_____

_____

READING FOR REAL

In small groups talk about the meaning of the words and *abbreviations* (short forms) below.

TERMS	MEANINGS	TERMS	MEANINGS
BA	bathroom	unfurnished	no furniture
BR	bedroom	&	and
condo	condominium	incl.	included
trailer	mobile home		

Exercise 3: Alex is still looking for a home to rent. He is reading ads in the newspaper. Read the ads. Then read the questions. Circle the correct answers.

1. What is the most expensive rental?
   a. the furnished apartment
   b. the unfurnished condo
   c. the house

2. What is the least expensive rental?
   a. the furnished apartment
   b. the unfurnished condo
   c. the mobile home

3. Which rental allows pets?
   a. the furnished apartment
   b. the unfurnished condo
   c. the mobile home

4. All four rental ads list
   a. the price.
   b. the location.
   c. the number of bedrooms.

5. None of the four rental ads lists
   a. the phone number.
   b. a pool.
   c. the local schools.

Apartment Furnished
Near downtown, pool
2 BR, 1.5 BA, nice furniture,
$650. Come and see!

Condo Unfurnished
$995, 2 BR 2 BA air/heat,
stove, refrig. 555-0039

House for Rent Unfurnished
Lakeside, $1295. Large 3 BR
2 BA, yard, garage. 555-9811

Mobile Home
$670 trailer & space, quiet,
pets OK, near shopping. Water
incl. $200 deposit. 555-4892

In Your Experience

In a group ask and answer these questions.

Why do some people like furnished rentals more than unfurnished rentals? Which of the four rentals do you like? Why?

In small groups talk about the words below.

daycare   license   tuberculosis   certificate

CULTURE CORNER

Your Own Family Daycare Business at Home

Do you want to earn money at home? A good way to earn money at home is to start your own business. Licensed family daycare is an excellent home business. You care for other people's children during the day while they work, and they pay you for the service. You can have up to eight children in your home. It can be fun, but you need to like working with children.

Read four sample rules. Remember, the rules can be different in each state.

1. Call the state licensing department to receive information on family daycare. Complete the papers for the license.

2. Be tested and get a certificate that says you do not have tuberculosis.

3. Ask the state department to come to check your home. You need a fire extinguisher. The home needs to be safe for children.

4. Take a health and safety course.

Your Turn

In a small group talk about family daycare. Ask these questions:

Do you know someone who has a family daycare business?
What is the price for each child?
Is daycare easy or hard work?

In Your Experience

Make a list of good and bad things about a business in your home.
Then in small groups talk about your ideas.
Make a list of everyone's ideas. Share the list with the class.

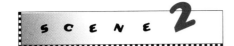

Bernard and Linda Brown want to buy a house.

Are you really sure? You won't change your mind?

Yes, I'm sure. I really like this house. Let's buy it.

I'll call our real estate agent right now.

We want to make an offer on the Orange Avenue house.

I'm sorry, it's sold. A woman bought it three hours ago.

FACTS   What did the Browns decide?

FEELINGS   How do you think the Browns feel about the news?

AND YOU?   Have you ever looked for a house or apartment?
             Was it easy or difficult?

SOUND BITES

The real estate agent is going to help the Browns look for another house.

Before You Listen With the class, talk about real estate agents.
Ask these questions.

> What do real estate agents do? How do they help people find homes?
> Who pays them? Is this a good job? Why or why not?

While You Listen Listen to the conversation between Linda Brown
and the real estate agent. Answer the questions about their plans
in your notebook.

> Who wants to make an appointment? What does Linda want to look at?
> When and where are Linda and the real estate agent going to meet?

After You Listen Real estate agents help people buy or
sell their homes. What kind of people make good agents?
Talk about your answer in a small group.

SPOTLIGHT ON FUTURE WITH *WILL*

I **will talk** to a real estate agent.   I **will not** talk to an agent.

I'**ll talk** to a real estate agent.   I **won't talk** to an agent.

I/You/He/She/We/They **will look** at townhouses.

I/You/He/She/We/They **won't look** at townhouses.

I'll = I will   *I won't = I will not*

Use *will* + verb to talk about the future.

Exercise 3: Finish the sentences with the words below and *will*, *'ll*, or *won't*. Use *won't* when you see the word *not*.

go   look at   be   see   drive   meet   need   stop

Linda (1) _____*will look at*_____ houses tomorrow.

She (2) _____ with Patty, the real estate agent.

She (3) _____ Patty at the office.

The appointment (4) _____ at 2:00.

Linda (5) _____ in Patty's car.

Linda (6) *not* _____ her car.

They (7) _____ different houses.

They (8) *not* _____ at apartments.

Person to Person

Listen to the conversations. Practice them with a partner.
Then change them to be true for you.

MR. DAVIS:	Where will we look at houses?	DAN:	I'll offer $98,000 for your house.
REAL ESTATE AGENT:	In the north part of town, near the river.	OWNER:	We won't take less than $100,000.
MR. DAVIS:	Oh, good. Will we see many today?	DAN:	Let me think about it.

Who is the real estate agent?   Patty is.

When is the appointment?   At 2:00 on Saturday.

Where are the houses?   In the north part of town.

What are the addresses?   1547 N. Maple St. and 533 6th St.

Why is Patty there?   She'll help show the houses.

How will they get there?   Patty will drive.

Use question words to find out information.

who = people   **when** = times   **where** = places

what = things   **why** = reasons   **how** = ways

When you speak, you can use the contractions *who's* (*who is*) and *when's* (*when is*).

VOCABULARY PROMPTS

In small groups talk about the meaning of the words and abbreviations below.

fireplace   open house   realty   gar.   sq. ft.   rm.   townhouse

Open House Sunday, 1:00–5:00.
Home in North Park neighborhood.
3 BR, 2 BA, with fireplace, patio.
Don't wait! Call Ofelia Gomez
Newton Realty 555-1737.

Townhouse located near Blue Lake
Open Sunday 1:00–4:00. Large living rm.,
quiet, view, 2 BR, 1.5 BA, 1 gar.
1000 sq. ft. $150,000.
Call Dora at Arrow Realty.

Exercise 4: Now look at the house ads.

Answer these questions about the two ads in your notebook.

1. When is the open house?
2. Where is the home?
3. Who is the real estate agent?
4. Why is this place special?
5. How can you get more information?

Your Turn

Find real estate ads in the paper. Ask a partner the questions above.

VOCABULARY PROMPTS

In small groups talk about the words below.

home-loan rate   monthly mortgage cost   cost of average home

GET GRAPHIC

Read this chart on housing information for the years 1988–1996.

HOUSING COSTS/ MORTGAGE RATES AND PAYMENTS

COST OF AVERAGE HOME		MONTHLY	
Year	in the United States	Home-Loan Rate	Mortgage Cost
1988	$90,000	9.3%	$591/month
1990	$97,000	10.0%	$673/month
1992	$103,700	8.1%	$615/month
1994	$109,800	7.5%	$612/month
1996	$122,700	7.9%	$715/month

Exercise 5: Circle the correct answer.

1. What year were average home costs highest?

    a. 1990   b. 1994   c. 1996

2. What year was the monthly payment highest?

    a. 1990   b. 1994   c. 1996

3. What year was the home-loan rate highest?

    a. 1990   b. 1994   c. 1996

4. What happened to the home-loan rate from 1988 to 1996?

    a. It went up.   b. It went up and then down.   c. It went down.

5. Look at the cost of an average home between 1988 and 1996.
   What do you think the cost will be in 1998?

    a. the same as in 1996   b. lower   c. higher

Your Turn

Use a newspaper to find the average rent of a two-bedroom house
or apartment in your area. Divide into three groups. Each group should
do these three things: List the rental cost for five two-bedroom rentals.
Find the average rental cost of these five homes. Compare lists and
average rents with other groups. What is the average rent of
a two-bedroom apartment in your area?

With a partner or a group talk about these words.

repair   decorate   investment

ISSUES AND ANSWERS

Alex and his son want to rent an apartment. Linda and Bernard
want to buy a house. They list their reasons below.
Which is better, to rent or buy?

REASONS TO RENT AN APARTMENT	REASONS TO BUY A HOUSE
You can move easily, without selling.	A house is an investment.
Renting can cost less money a month.	You can decorate your way.
The manager or owner will repair broken things.	You will have the home for the future.
You don't have to take care of the yard.	You can stay there as long as you want.

Now write two more reasons on each list.

_____   _____

_____   _____

Your Turn

With a partner talk about the six reasons to rent and the six reasons to buy.
Choose the best reason from each list.
Each partner should read one best reason to the class.
Make a class list of reasons.
The class will vote on the three best reasons to rent.
Then the class will vote on the three best reasons to buy.
Make a class chart or list with the six reasons.

WRAP-UP

Make an idea map with questions and answers about your dream house or apartment. Write four more questions in the circles below.
Use *how many, how much, who, when, where,* or *what.*
Then write answers to the six questions.

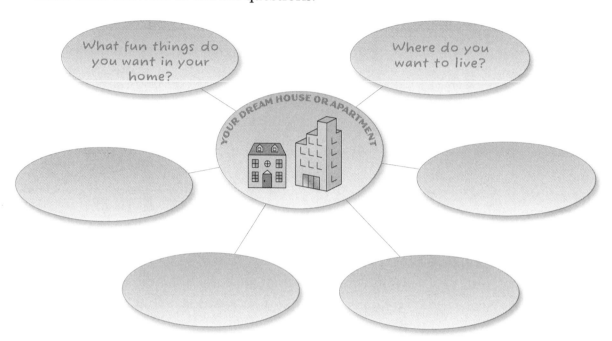

What fun things do you want in your home?

Where do you want to live?

YOUR DREAM HOUSE OR APARTMENT

Think About Learning

In this unit you learned a variety of skills and language structures. Look at the items in the list below and check how easy or difficult each item was for you. At the bottom write one other thing you learned.

SKILLS / STRUCTURES	Page	easy ☺	so-so 😐	difficult ☹
Talk about people's problems	62			
Understand housing ads	65			
Read a chart	70			
Read about reasons to rent or buy	71			
Use an idea map	72			
Use *how much/how many*	63			
Use future with *will*	68			
Use question words	69			

GETTING AROUND:
PUBLIC AND PRIVATE
TRANSPORTATION

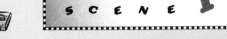

S C E N E 1

Talk about the pictures with a partner.
Ask each other the questions below.
Share your answers with another pair or the class.

Bassam is taking the bus to a job interview.
He has a five dollar bill.

FACTS   What did Bassam give the driver? What's the problem?

FEELINGS   How does Bassam feel about going to get change?

AND YOU?   Do you take the bus? When do you need exact change?
Where do you get change?

VOCABULARY PROMPTS

Before you listen, read the words below with a partner.
Talk about them with the class.

transit center   cross street   transfer   exact change

SOUND BITES

Listen to these conversations about taking the bus.

While You Listen Read the questions. Circle *yes* or *no* to answer them.

Conversation 1

1. The caller lives on Market Street.   yes   no
2. The caller is on Vermont Street.   yes   no
3. Does the caller know the name
   of the cross street?   yes   no

Conversation 2

4. The bus ride cost $1.65.   yes   no
5. The driver gave change.   yes   no

Conversation 3

6. The woman paid another 35 cents.   yes   no
7. She got a transfer for bus 10.   yes   no

After You Listen Share your answers with a partner or small group.
Then talk with your teacher and the whole class.
In your area how much do you pay for a bus transfer?

SPOTLIGHT ON *NEED TO* AND *HAVE TO*

Need to + verb

I / You / We / They	**need to wait for**	the bus.
I / You / We / They	**do not need to take**	the bus.
He / She	**needs to call**	transit information.
He / She	**doesn't need to get**	change.

Have to + verb

I / You / We / They	**have to walk**	home.
I / You / We / They	**don't have to go**	now.
He / She	**has to call**	a taxi.
He / She	**doesn't have to ride**	a bicycle.

Need to + verb and *have to* + verb mean the same thing.
They show obligation or responsibility.

Exercise 1: Look at the picture. Read the story.

Bertha Washington is a bus driver. She drives bus number 12 every day. She has to work from 7:00 A.M. to 3:00 P.M. She needs to watch the traffic in the street. She needs to watch people pay money and to give them transfer tickets. She is responsible for the bus and the passengers. Bus drivers need to be careful and responsible. They have to watch everything!

Your Turn

Write three things Bertha has to do in her job.
She is responsible for these things.

_____

_____

_____

VOCABULARY PROMPTS

Talk about these words and phrases in small groups.

a ride   low on gas   exit   pharmacy   cash a check

Person to Person

Look at the pictures and listen to the conversations. Talk about them with a partner. With your partner finish the last conversation. Use *need to* or *have to*.

PABLO: Excuse me, Mr. Smith, I have a problem.

MR. SMITH: What's wrong?

PABLO: I feel sick. I need to go home.

MR. SMITH: That's too bad. Go home, Pablo, but please call me early tomorrow morning and tell me how you feel.

PABLO: Thanks for the ride. I feel really sick.

MARTIN: No problem. Where do you need to go?

PABLO: To Smart-Buy pharmacy. It's at Market and Adams.

MARTIN: Which way is that?

PABLO: You have to turn left at the corner. Then get on Route 22 and exit at Market Street.

PAMELA: Hi, Mark. Can you give me a ride to work tonight?

MARK: Well, my car is low on gas. Do you have some money for gas?

PAMELA: Sure, I need to cash a check, and then I can give you five dollars. OK?

MARK: Great. That helps. See you at 5:30.

KATE: Can I borrow your bicycle?

MIKE: Where are you going?

KATE: _____

             _____

VOCABULARY PROMPTS

Read the words and talk about them with your class.

responsibility   cause   brake lights   rear end   damaged

READING FOR REAL

Read about accident reports.

DEPENDABLE INSURANCE CO.

Martin Ramirez
617 Washington Ave.
Dallas, TX 75204

Policy Number
0623 294636

Expiration Date
7/31/02

Vehicle ID Number
3B3EF47COTS626599

Year/Make/Model
97 Ford Escort

If you have an automobile accident, you have to call the police and make a report. This is your responsibility. You need to show your driver's license to the police officer. In many states you also have to show your insurance card.

At 1:30 A.M. Pablo's friend Martin had an acccident on Lemon Street in Dallas, Texas. He did not see the brake lights of the car in front of him. He hit the rear end of that car. Both cars were damaged, but no one was hurt. Martin called the police. A police officer came and asked him and the other driver questions about the accident.

Exercise 2: Work with a partner. Write the answers in your notebook. Then, with your partner role-play the conversation between the police officer and Martin. One student is the police officer. The other student is Martin. The officer asks and Martin answers.

Police Officer	Martin
1. Can I see your driver's license?	Yes, officer, here it is.
2. Was anyone hurt?	
3. What happened?	
4. What time did the accident happen?	
5. Where did the accident happen?	

In Your Experience

In small groups talk about the answers to these questions.

Do you have to have proof of insurance in your state?
Is this a good idea? Why or why not?
Share your ideas with the class.

In a small group talk about the words and look at the pictures below.
Ask your teacher if you need help.

seat belt   passenger

child safety seat

breath test   alcohol

proof of insurance

 ## CULTURE CORNER

Read the information about driving rules.

In California, car drivers have to follow some important rules. All other states
in the United States have rules too. Here are a few of the California rules.

1. Seat belts   All drivers and passengers of cars and trucks have to
   wear seat belts at all times.

2. Children   All children under two years old have to sit in a child safety
   seat with a seat belt.

3. Insurance   All cars, trucks, and motorcycles need to have insurance for
   accidents. Drivers need to have proof of insurance with them.

4. Breath test   The police can ask drivers to take a breath test.
   The breath test checks for alcohol.

  Your Turn

These rules are your responsibility if you drive. What happens if you
don't follow the rules? Talk with your class and your teacher.
Then write other rules for drivers in your state on large paper or on the board.

 In Your Experience

Are these rules like the rules for drivers in your country?
Write your answer in your notebook or talk about it in a small group.

 Talk about the pictures with a partner.
Ask each other the questions below.
Share your answers with another pair or the class.

> Excuse me, what time is the bus coming?

> Which bus are you waiting for?

> Bus number 7.

> Oh, it comes every hour on the hour. It's coming again in 45 minutes, at 12:00.

> I hate waiting for buses! They're so slow!

FACTS What is Bassam waiting for? What's the problem?

FEELINGS How does he feel?

AND YOU? Do you take public transportation?
How long do you wait for public transportation every week?

SOUND BITES

Bassam is talking to his friends Jamal and Lilia about
going to work and going to a rock concert.

Before You Listen With a partner list all the different types
of transportation in your city.

While You Listen Using your list, make a check mark next to the
transportation that Bassam and his friends are talking about.

After You Listen Share your opinions with the class.

What kind of public transportation is there in your area?
Is there enough public transportation in your area? Why or why not?
Do you prefer to go by car or by public transportation?

SPOTLIGHT ON PRESENT CONTINUOUS

Am / is / are + a verb ending in *-ing* show an action that is happening now.

Are you **studying** English this year?   Yes, I **am**.

Is Lilia **going** to the grocery store?   No, she**'s not**. She**'s going** to the mall.

Am / is / are + a verb ending in *-ing* can also tell about an action that will happen soon.

Are you **coming** to the dance tomorrow?   Yes, I **am**.
Is Pablo **walking** to work today?   No, he **isn't**. He**'s taking** the bus.

Exercise 2: Write answers to these questions.
Use present continuous.

1. Are you looking for a job now?

_____

2. Are you taking the bus home from school today?

_____

3. Are you walking home after class today?

_____

4. Are you staying home this weekend?

_____

Person to Person

Listen to these conversations. Practice them with a partner.
Then change them to be true for you.

HENRY: Do you want a ride to work tomorrow, Lori?

LORI: Maybe. What time are you leaving?

HENRY: I'm leaving my house at 7:15.

TOM: When are you going home tonight?

SUSAN: At 8:30. What about you?

TOM: I'm not going home until 9:00.

SPOTLIGHT ON *COULD* AND *WOULD* FOR REQUESTS

Questions

Could you give me a ride?

Would you hand me that map, **please**?

Would you **please** help me?

Possible Answers

Affirmative: Of course. / Yes. / Sure. / No problem.

Negative: No, I can't. / Sorry, I can't.

You can use *could* and *would* to form polite requests.

You can add *please* to make a request even more polite.

VOCABULARY PROMPTS

Talk about these words with your class.

break down   dispatcher   tow truck

Exercise 3: Bassam's car broke down on the highway earlier this week. He called for a tow truck. With a partner complete his conversation. Use *could*, *would* and *please*.

DISPATCHER: Hello, Anderson Towing. Can I help you?

BASSAM: Yes, (1) _____ you send a tow truck to tow

my car? It broke down on Highway 8.

DISPATCHER: (2) _____ you tell me your exact location,

(3) _____?

BASSAM: I'm on Highway 8 near Exit 123. (4) _____

you (5) _____ hurry?

DISPATCHER: We'll try, but we're pretty busy. You're going to have to wait
at least 30 minutes.

Your Turn

Role-play the conversation with your partner.

GET GRAPHIC

Read the story, study the tables, and answer the questions.

Maxine just got the job of her dreams in Los Angeles. So next week she has to take the Metrolink train to work from her home in Irvine to Los Angeles and back again. The company she'll work for is just one block from Los Angeles's Union Station. She needs to be at work by 8:45 A.M. She'll leave work at 4:45 P.M.

Maxine stopped at the Irvine train station today and got information about schedules and routes.
She needs to study the information in the tables carefully.

TO LOS ANGELES	A.M.					P.M.
TRAIN NUMBERS	601	603	681	683	605	701
Oceanside	4:51	5:26			6:45	
San Clemente	5:11	5:47			7:06	
San Juan Capistrano	5:20	5:56			7:15	
Irvine	5:32	6:09	6:40	7:09	7:29	
Santa Ana	5:42	6:19	6:51	7:21	7:40	
Orange	5:47	6:24	6:56	7:26	7:45	
Anaheim	5:51	6:28	7:00	7:30	7:49	
Fullerton	5:59	6:36	7:09	7:39	7:57	6:22
Norwalk/Santa Fe Springs	6:08	6:45	7:18	7:48	8:06	6:32
Commerce		6:53			8:14	
L.A. Union Station	6:36	7:16	7:46	8:16	8:38	7:13

FROM LOS ANGELES	A.M.	P.M.					
TRAIN NUMBERS	700	682	686	604	688	606	608
L.A. Union Station	6:49	2:50	3:32	4:35	4:55	5:37	6:26
Commerce		3:06		4:51		5:53	
Norwalk/Santa Fe Springs	7:13	3:16	3:55	5:01	5:21	6:03	6:49
Fullerton	7:27	3:25	4:04	5:10	5:30	6:12	6:58
Anaheim		3:33	4:12	5:18	5:38	6:20	7:07
Orange		3:37	4:16	5:22	5:42	6:24	7:11
Santa Ana		3:41	4:22	5:26	5:48	6:28	7:15
Irvine		3:54	4:35	5:37	6:01	6:39	7:26
San Juan Capistrano			4:49	5:49		6:52	7:38
San Clemente				6:01		7:04	7:50
Oceanside				6:26		7:29	8:15

1. What time does Maxine need to get on the train in Irvine? _____

2. What time will she arrive in L.A.'s Union Station? _____

3. How long will her ride be? _____

4. What time will she return to Irvine? _____

5. When is the last train she can take to return to Irvine? _____

Your Turn

With a partner plan a trip using the train schedule above.
Start from Maxine's home in Irvine and choose a destination.
Write the answers to the questions below in your notebook.

Where do you want to go? What time are you going to leave?
How much time will it take? When are you going to come home?

Talk about the words below with your classmates and teacher.
Then read about new and used cars.

factory warranty   technology   registration

ISSUES AND ANSWERS

Bob and Ray are talking about buying a car.
Bob is in favor of buying a new car.
Ray is in favor of buying a used car. Here's what they say.

Bob wants a new car because

1. a new car has a longer life.

2. a new car has a factory warranty.

3. a new car has the best technology.

Ray prefers a used car because

1. a used car costs much less than a new car.

2. insurance costs less for a used car.

3. registration costs less for a used car.

In Your Experience

In a group talk about your own experience buying a car.
Then complete the sentences with your ideas or the group's ideas.

1. I think a good thing about a new car is _____

_____

2. I think a bad thing about a new car is _____

_____

3. I think a good thing about a used car is _____

_____

4. I think a bad thing about a used car is _____

_____

WRAP-UP

With a partner complete the T-chart below. A T-chart helps you think and write. Write the *advantages* (*good things*) of public transportation on the left side. Write the *disadvantages* (*bad things*) of public transportation on the right.

PUBLIC TRANSPORTATION ADVANTAGES	PUBLIC TRANSPORTATION DISADVANTAGES

Think About Learning

In this unit you learned a variety of skills and language structures. Look at the list below and check how easy or difficult each item was for you. At the bottom write one other thing you learned.

SKILLS / STRUCTURES	Page	easy ☺	so-so 😐	difficult ☹
Talk about getting around	79			
Read about a bus driver's job	75			
Report an accident	77			
Learn about rules for cars	78			
Read a graph	82			
Complete a T-chart	84			
Use *have to* and *need to*	75			
Use present continuous	80			
Use *could* and *would* for requests	81			

Unit 8

Your Library and Other Community Services

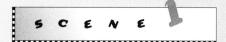
S C E N E 1

Talk about the pictures with a partner.
Ask each other the questions below.
Share your answers with another pair or the class.

Steve and Pedro are talking at break time.

> Steve, I want to go to interesting places, but I don't have much money. What should I do?

> You should go to Japan! You should visit Mexico! You should see the world!

> With a credit card?

> No, with a library card!

FACTS   What is Pedro's problem? What is Steve's solution?

FEELINGS   How does Pedro feel? How does Steve feel?

AND YOU?   Do you like to read? Do you have a library card?
               Can a book be like a vacation?
               Can you visit another country with a video?

Before you listen, talk about the words below with a partner.

library

park

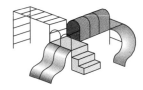

playground

clinic

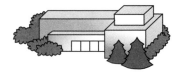

school

SOUND BITES

Pedro thinks his family stays home too much.
He's talking about places in the community.

While You Listen Write the place on the line below.
Use the words in the Vocabulary Prompts
at the top of the page.

1. Pedro's mother should go to the ___park.___.

2. Pedro's sister should go to the _____.

3. Pedro's nephew should go to the _____.

4. Pedro's niece should go to the _____.

5. Pedro's grandfather should go to a _____.

After You Listen Check your answers with a partner.

Your Turn

With your partner ask and answer questions about Pedro's family
and places in the community. Here's an example.

PARTNER 1:   Where should Pedro's mother go?

PARTNER 2:   She should go to the park.

PARTNER 1:   Why?

PARTNER 2:   Because she stays home too much.

You **should** go to the library.
You **shouldn't** stay home.

I / You / He / She / We / You / They **should** read more.
I / You / He / She / We / You / They **shouldn't** watch so much TV.

shouldn't = should not
Use *should* to give advice or express an opinion.
Use *shouldn't* to tell what not to do.

Exercise 1: Steve is trying to help Pedro. He checks to make sure he understands the problems in Pedro's family. Copy the story in your notebook. Complete Steve's sentences with *should* or *shouldn't*.

Your mother stays in the house too much. She (1) _____

take a walk in the park. Your grandfather (2) _____ go to school

because he needs to make friends and learn English. And he

(3) _____ watch so much TV. Your nephew sits and plays

video games too much. He (4) _____ go to the playground

to play with other kids his age. Your brother-in-law smokes cigarettes

all day. He (5) _____ smoke so much. Your sister

(6) _____ see the doctor at the clinic because she is pregnant.

She (7) _____ work so hard. And you want to visit interesting places.

You (8) _____ come to the library with me!

Your Turn

Read Steve's sentences to a partner.
Make a list of the community places you find in Steve's sentences.
With a partner, check your list and add two more places from
your community. Share the new places with another pair of students.
Give advice using *should* and *shouldn't* and the names of the places.
For example, say, "You should use the bank.
You shouldn't keep all your money in the house."

Talk about the words below in a small group.

disabled   elderly   litter   flu shots

Person to Person

Talk to a partner about each sign. Say, for example, "Where is the first sign from?" Your partner should answer, "It's from the library." Then listen to the conversations. With your partner, finish the last conversation. Use *should* or *shouldn't*. Then practice the conversations.

A: Wow! The library has videos too!

B: Shhh. You shouldn't talk so loud!

A: Oh, sorry. I forgot.

A: Excuse me, miss. You shouldn't sit in the front seat.

B: What? Oh, I'm sorry. I didn't see the sign.

A: That's OK.

BUS PASSENGERS

Front Seats for Disabled and Elderly Persons

A: The park is beautiful!

B: Yes, but people shouldn't litter. Someone left that paper bag on the ground.

A: We should put it in the trash.

A: Did you read the sign?

B: _____

_____

CLINIC NEWS

Get **FREE** flu shots next month

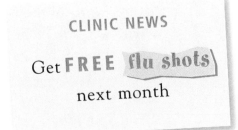

Your Turn

With a partner, present one conversation for the class.

VOCABULARY PROMPTS

Talk about these words in a small group.

guardian   application   ID card   social security card

 ## READING FOR REAL

Steve and Pedro are at the public library.
Pedro is reading the information about getting a library card.

Spring Valley Public Library

HOW TO GET A LIBRARY CARD

1 **Fill out Part A of the application.** Write your name, address, telephone number, social security number, and native language. Sign your name.

2 **Complete Part B if you are under 16 years old.** Write your date of birth. Have a parent or guardian sign the form.

3 **Give your application to a librarian.** Show the librarian a social security card, ID card, or driver's license.

4 **Show the librarian proof of residence, something that shows your address.** Bring a bill with your name and address on it, or an envelope with a canceled stamp and your name and address.

Exercise 2: In a small group ask and answer these questions.

1. What information should Pedro write in Part A of the library card application?

2. Pedro is 22 years old. Should he fill out Part B of the application?

3. Why should Pedro bring his ID card and a telephone bill with him to the library?

4. Do you think it is easy or difficult to get a library card? Explain.

  Your Turn

In class take a survey. Ask these questions.
How many students have library cards? How many use them?
One or two students—or your teacher—should go to the library
and get applications for the class to complete.

VOCABULARY PROMPTS

In small groups talk about the words below.

freedom   celebrate   rights   speech   press

CULTURE CORNER

Pedro and Steve see this sign in the library. Read the sign.
Then read the information about freedom and the Constitution.

Freedom is important to Americans.
Two kinds of freedom are *freedom of speech* (people can say what they want) and *freedom of the press* (people can write and read what they want). All people living in the United States have these freedoms. The First Amendment to the Constitution of the United States gives Americans these freedoms. The Constitution tells Americans what they can and cannot do in their country. It is the most important law in the country.

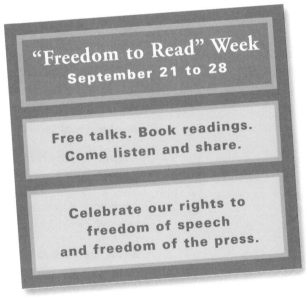

"Freedom to Read" Week
September 21 to 28

Free talks. Book readings.
Come listen and share.

Celebrate our rights to
freedom of speech
and freedom of the press.

Exercise 3: Think about the questions. Write answers in your notebook.

1. At this library why is the week of September 21 to 28 special?
2. What can people do at the library that week?
3. What is freedom of speech? freedom of the press?
4. What gives people in the United States these freedoms?
5. Why should libraries celebrate freedom?

In Your Experience

In a group ask and answer these questions. Then share your answers with the class.

Should adults be able to say, read, and write anything they want to?
Should children be able to say, read, and write anything they want to?
Is there freedom of speech and the press in your native country?
What books, magazines, and newspapers are important to you? Why?

In the library, Pedro asks the librarian for help.

What's this computer for?

This computer can help you find things in the library.

What's that computer for?

Oh, that's the Internet computer. That computer can help you find information from all over the world!

FACTS   What do you see in the picture?

FEELINGS   How do you think Pedro feels?

AND YOU?   Do you have a library in your community?
           Do you go to the library? Why or why not?

VOCABULARY PROMPTS

Before you listen, talk about the words below with the class.

computerized catalog	Internet computer	reference books	videotapes
children's books	magazines	cassette tapes	
dictionaries	adult-literacy books	newspapers	

SOUND BITES

Pedro and the librarian are talking about the library.

While You Listen In the Vocabulary Prompts above, put a check (✔) next to the words you hear.

After You Listen Share answers with a partner.

SPOTLIGHT ON DEMONSTRATIVE PRONOUNS

THIS, THAT, THESE, AND THOSE

Singular

This is a book.

That's a book.

Plural

These are magazines.

Those are magazines.

Use *this* and *these* to talk about something nearby.

Use *that* and *those* to talk about something far away.

That's = *That is* There are no other contractions for these four words.

Exercise 4: What is Pedro saying? Circle the correct answer.

1. This is a computer for the librarian.

   That's a computer for students.

2. This is an English dictionary.

   That's a Spanish dictionary.

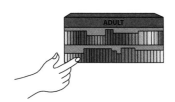

3. These are children's books.

   Those are books for adults.

4. These are videotapes for adults.

   Those are videotapes for children.

Person to Person

Listen to the conversation. Practice it with a partner.
Then change it to be true for you.

STEVE: Pedro, I see you have some things from the library.
What's that? And what are those?

PEDRO: This is a videotape for my nephew, and these are books
for my mother.

STEVE: Great!

SPOTLIGHT ON THE DEMONSTRATIVE ADJECTIVES
THIS, THAT, THESE, AND THOSE

Singular

This section is for children.

Singular

That section is for adults.

Plural

These books are for children.

Plural

Those books are for adults.

Use *this*, *that*, *these*, and *those* before nouns. Use *this* and *these* to show something is near.
Use *that* and *those* to show something is far away.

Exercise 5: Complete the sentences. Use *this*, *that*, *these*, and *those*.

1. _____ book is about Mexico.

2. _____ book is about Alaska.

3. _____ tapes are for children.

4. _____ tapes are for adults.

Your Turn

In your notebook write four sentences about your class
or your classroom. Use the demonstrative adjectives.
Use *is* and *are*. For example, write, "That desk is for my teacher"
or "These students are from Mexico."

GET GRAPHIC

The U.S. Department of Education asked people about reading and about their weekly pay. Look at the bar graph. What does the graph tell you about good readers? about poor readers?

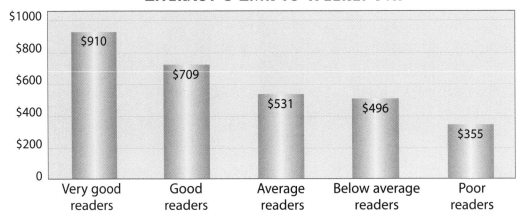

LITERACY'S LINK TO WEEKLY PAY

Exercise 6: Complete the sentences.

1. Poor readers earn $ _____ a week.

2. Very good readers earn $ _____ a week.

3. Average readers earn $ _____ a week.

4. Good readers earn $ _____ a week.

5. Below average readers earn $ _____ a week.

Your Turn

The sentence below explains the bar graph. Complete the sentence. Use the words *good readers* and *poor readers*.

This bar graph shows that _____ make more

money than _____.

In Your Experience

In a group answer these questions.

Do you like to read? Why or why not?
What do you read in your native language?
What do you read in English?
Do you have to read at your job?
Why do good readers earn more than poor readers?

ISSUES AND ANSWERS

Read the suggestions and the answers below.

LIBRARY SUGGESTION BOX

SUGGESTION 1

I don't know how to use computers. You have many computers in the library. But you should help people use them.

LIBRARIAN'S ANSWER 1

Ask the librarian to help you. If the librarian is busy, please wait. Also, you can bring a friend, and you can help each other. After you learn the computer, teach your friend. Working together is a good idea. And remember, you can always ask for help!

SUGGESTION 2

Do you sometimes sell old library books? You should have a book sale.

LIBRARIAN'S ANSWER 2

We do! We have book sales many times a year. We put used books out on tables for you to buy. Sometimes we also have free magazines. You should ask the librarian about the free magazines. And you should ask about the next book sale too!

In a small group talk about suggestions 1 and 2. Write two questions to ask a librarian. Ask about computers, books, or other things. Share your questions with the group. Together, pick the two best questions to share with the class.

Question 1 _____

Question 2 _____

WRAP-UP

Sue is new to the United States. She has three children, but she doesn't have much money. Where should she and her children go in the community? With a group finish the idea map. Use *should*.

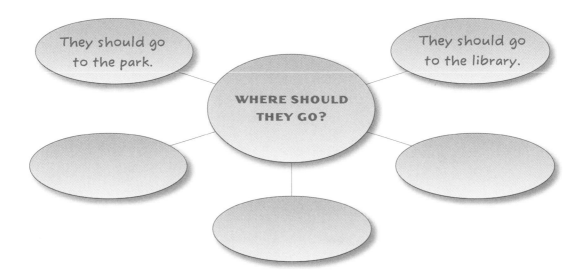

They should go to the park.

They should go to the library.

WHERE SHOULD THEY GO?

With your group choose the best place for Sue and her children to go. Then tell why it is the best place. Write your answer on a paper or the board. Present your group's answer to the class.

Think About Learning

In this unit you learned a variety of skills and language structures. Look at the items in the list below and check how easy or difficult each item was for you. At the bottom write one other thing you learned.

SKILLS / STRUCTURES	Page	easy ☺	so-so 😐	difficult ☹
Understand and talk about the library and other places in the community	86, 88			
Learn how to get a library card	89			
Talk about freedoms in the United States	90			
Read a bar graph	94			
Talk about and solve problems	85, 86			
Use an idea map	96			
Use *should* and *shouldn't*	87			
Use *this, that, these,* and *those*	92, 93			

THE JOB SEARCH

Talk about the pictures with a partner. Ask each other the
questions below. Share your answers with another pair or the class.

Manolo saw an interesting help-wanted ad for a general office worker.
He called about the ad, and the Human Resources Manager asked
him to come in for an interview.

> Manolo, can you use a computer?

> Yes, I can use a computer, and I can operate a cash register too.

> Can you work on the weekends?

> No, I can't. I can't work on Saturdays, and I can't work on Sundays either.

> I have a question. Can employees here start early and leave early?

> No, you can't leave before 5:00, and you can't come in very early either. The office is closed before 9:00.

FACTS   What is happening?

FEELINGS   How do you think the boss feels?
How do you think Manolo feels at the end of the interview?

AND YOU?   Do you have a job? If so, what was your interview like?
How many interviews did you have before you got the job?
How did you feel?

SOUND BITES

Before You Listen In a group look at chart 1 and talk about the job skills. Help your group understand the words in the chart. Then look at chart 2 and talk about the words for job rules.

While You Listen Listen to the conversations about skills and jobs. For each chart put a check (✔) next to what each person can do.

CHART 1

Skills	Tony	Lawanda	Siu	Alfredo
Use a computer				
Repair automobiles				
Drive a truck				
Lift heavy loads				
Type 60 words per minute				

CHART 2

Job Policies	Yes	No
Start work early and leave early		
Take a sick day with pay		
Use the company car		
Take off an hour for lunch		

After You Listen Now decide which person is best for these jobs. With a partner compare your answers.

1. mechanic _____

2. administrative assistant _____

3. warehouse worker _____

4. truck driver _____

SPOTLIGHT ON MEANINGS OF *CAN* AND *CAN'T*

Ability/Skills

Statements

I/You/He/She/We/They **can** type.
                      can't

Questions

Can you type?

Giving Permission

You **can** take this book.

Asking for Permission

Can I smoke?

Refusing Permission/Expressing Rules

You **can't** smoke here.
              leave work early.

Use *can* and *can't* to talk about skills and ability.

In spoken English you can also use *can* and *can't* to ask for, give, and refuse permission.

Exercise 1: In your notebook write four sentences about your job skills—what you can and can't do. Then tell a partner. For example, write, "I can speak Spanish. I can't use a computer."

Exercise 2: In a group think about school rules—what you can and can't do at school. Make a list and share your list with the class. For example, write, "At this school you can come to class late, but you can't copy your classmates' answers on a test."

Person to Person

Listen to the conversation. With a partner complete the conversation. Then practice it with a partner.

A: Tell me about your job skills. Can you use a computer?

B: Yes, I can.

A: That's good. What about your language skills? Can you speak Spanish?

B: Yes I can. And I can speak French too.

A: Really? That's great. Can you speak any other languages?

B: No I can't. I speak English, Spanish, and French.

A: That's really good. Well, those are my questions. Do you have any questions for me?

B: _____.

_____.

SPOTLIGHT ON COMPOUND SENTENCES WITH *AND . . . TOO* AND *AND . . . EITHER*

Affirmative Sentences

I can use a computer, **and** I can communicate well **too**.

José landscapes, **and** he cleans houses **too**.

Negative Sentences

I can't work evenings, **and** I can't work weekends **either**.

They can't pay a mechanic, **and** they can't repair their car **either**.

Use *and . . . too* to combine two affirmative sentences.

Use *and . . . either* to combine two negative sentences.

Exercise 3: Join the sentences. Talk with a partner.
Use the box above for help. For example, for number 1 say,
"Lawanda can drive a car, and she can drive a truck too."

1. Lawanda can drive a car. She can drive a truck.
2. Alfredo is strong. He is a hard worker.
3. Tony can't type well. He can't communicate well with others.
4. Nora and Joseph don't have a computer. They don't have a typewriter.
5. Mohammed can come to work early. He can leave early.
6. Komiko doesn't take an hour for lunch. She doesn't leave the office.

Your Turn

Write two affirmative or two negative sentences about yourself.

1. _____

   _____

2. _____

   _____

Exercise 4: Find a partner. Your partner will join your sentences.
Write what your partner says.

1. _____

   _____

2. _____

   _____

VOCABULARY PROMPTS

With a partner talk about the words below.

appropriate clothes

job application

firm handshake

honest and positive

READING FOR REAL

Manolo's friend John saw this article in the newspaper.
He thinks the job interview tips can help Manolo get a job.
Read the tips from the newspaper.

JOB INTERVIEW TIPS

Before the Interview:

Think about the questions on a job application. Bring information to answer the questions. You should have names, addresses, and telephone numbers from your old jobs and schools too. Practice speaking about the application information with a friend. Answer questions about your job experience and job skills. Before you leave your home, you should be clean and neat. Wear appropriate clothes.

At the Interview:

Look happy. Smile. Stand straight. Give a firm handshake. Look in the interviewer's eyes when you speak. Don't be shy. Learn and use the interviewer's name. Ask questions when you don't understand. Be honest and positive. If the answer to a question is "no," don't lie and say "yes." You should always tell the truth. Add a few good words about yourself too. For example: "Can you use a computer?" "Not yet, but I can learn. I go to school, and my teacher says I'm a fast learner."

  Talk About It

Review the tip sentences with your partner. Write two or three key words from each tip. Then close your book. Use the key words to talk about each tip sentence. Now give all the tips. Your partner can help by giving you a key word.

 Your Turn

Role-play a tip sentence with your partner. The class will guess which tip it is.

VOCABULARY PROMPTS

In a small group talk about the words below.

corporation   successful   ball girl   give up   recipe

CULTURE CORNER

Read a true story about an American businesswoman.

DEBBI FIELDS, BUSINESSWOMAN

Debbi Fields is a famous businesswoman. She owns shops that sell delicious fresh-baked cookies. Her corporation is worth 100 million dollars. It has 600 shops all over the world.

Debbi wasn't always so successful. At age 13 she was a ball girl for a baseball team. Later she was a store clerk. When she was 20, she decided to sell cookies. People said selling cookies was a bad idea. Debbi didn't give up. She opened her first store in Palo Alto, California, in 1977.

Mrs. Fields wanted to spend more time at home with her five daughters. She made an office in her home. She says she learned a lot about business through her family. She learned about time management, people management, and caring for others.

Source: AP/Wide World Photos

Exercise 5: Circle *a* or *b*.

1. Debbi Fields is famous for
   a. her cookies.
   b. her first store.

2. Mrs. Fields cookies
   a. are in 600 shops in the world.
   b. are still not well known.

3. Debbi's first job was as a
   a. ball girl for a baseball team.
   b. store clerk.

4. Debbi didn't give up
   a. her job as a clerk.
   b. her plan to sell cookies.

5. She had an office at home
   a. to have more space.
   b. to be with her family.

Your Turn

Answer the questions below with a partner. Share your answers with the class. What are some things Debbi learned before opening her business? What other things should someone opening a business know?

Talk about the pictures with a partner.
Ask each other the questions below.
Share your answers with another pair or the class.

> **Come in and fill out an application.**

> **OK. Can I come in on Tuesday?**

> **No. Applications must be in by Monday. We have a lot of applicants, so you should even come in today.**

> **Paco, I need new clothes for an interview. But I won't have any money before Tuesday!**

> **Don't worry. I'll lend you some money.**

FACTS   What do you see? What is Manolo talking about on the phone?

FEELINGS   How does Manolo feel? Does he want the job?
Does he want to fill out an application today? Why or why not?

AND YOU?   How do you feel about job applications and interviews?
When did you last fill out a job application?

SOUND BITES

Manolo bought some new clothes and filled out an application.
The Human Resources Manager called for an interview.

Before You Listen Look at the list in the next section.
In a group talk about the words you don't know.

While You Listen Check which things Manolo has to do by next Monday.

_____ find people to recommend him _____ take a drug test

_____ give references to the company _____ fill out paycheck forms

After You Listen Check your answers with the group.
Do you have the same answers? With the class talk about the answers.

SPOTLIGHT ON *MUST* AND *MUST NOT*

I / You / He / She / We / They   **must** provide three references.

The references   **must not** be relatives.

Must has the same form for all persons.

Use *must* in formal contexts to express obligation.

Must in the affirmative means "have to."

Must not means "It is not permitted."

Exercise 6: Read the chart from the company policy manual.
Fill in the blanks with *must* or *must not*.

> **DRUGS**
>
> 1. Company employees _____ be drug free.
>
> 2. Applicants _____ take a drug test prior to employment.
>
> 3. Employees _____ take or sell drugs at the company or elsewhere.
>
> **HOURS**
>
> 1. Employees _____ be on time for work.
>
> 2. Employees _____ leave early.
>
> 3. Employees _____ take more than an hour for lunch.
>
> 4. Employees _____ phone the company in case of illness.

Your Turn

Write sentences in your notebook about rules at school.
Use *must* and *must not*. For example, write, "Students must not
be late for class."

Person to Person

Listen to the conversation. Practice it with a partner.
Then change it to be true for you.

JORGE:	I'm interested in a job as a taxi driver.
TAXI COMPANY:	You must have a driver's license for that job.
JORGE:	I'm applying for my driver's license now. Is that OK?
TAXI COMPANY:	What kind of license are you getting?
JORGE:	I don't know, a regular driver's license.
TAXI COMPANY:	All taxi drivers must have a Class B driver's license.

SPOTLIGHT ON *MUST* AND *HAVE TO*

Must and *Have to*

You **must** provide three references.   = You **have to** provide three references.

Must not

Your references **must not** be relatives.   = It is not permitted to use relatives as references.

Don't have to

You **don't have to** take the drug test twice.   = You don't need to take it twice.

In the affirmative, *must* and *have to* are almost the same; *must* is more formal.
The negative is very different: use *must not* to mean something is not permitted;
use *don't have to* to mean something is not necessary.

Exercise 7: With a partner complete the conversation with *must, must not, have to,* or *don't/doesn't have to*. Use the negative form when you see (*not*).

PERSONNEL: Applications for the office clerk job _____ be in by 5:00.

FRANÇOIS: _____ I _____ give you the names of references today?

PERSONNEL: Yes. All applicants _____

give three references. And the references _____

be on the application.

FRANÇOIS: OK. Then should I call about the job next week?

PERSONNEL: If you want to, but you (*not*) _____ call.

We'll call you.

FRANÇOIS: _____ I _____

do anything else?

PERSONNEL: No, that's it.

Your Turn

With your partner role-play the conversation.

VOCABULARY PROMPTS

With a partner or a group, talk about the words below. These words are in the bar graph. If you find a word you don't know, ask your teacher.

résumé   percentage   bilingual   attitude

GET GRAPHIC

Manolo found this bar graph in a newspaper.
It tells what skills and qualities employers want new employees to have.

WHAT EMPLOYERS IN OUR TOWN WANT

Employers want new employees with the following:

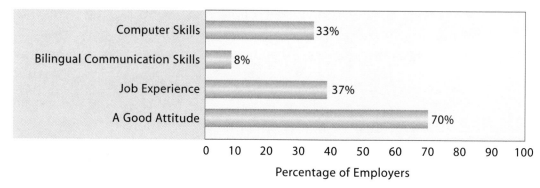

Percentage of Employers

Exercise 8: Give the correct answer according to the information in the graph.

1. On this bar graph, the numbers 0 to 100 are

   a. percentages.   b. dollars.   c. employees.

2. Write the percentage of employers requiring

   a. computer skills _____   b. bilingual skills _____

   c. experience _____   d. a good attitude _____

3. What do employers want most? second? third? fourth?
   Write 1, 2, 3, and 4.

   a. computer skills _____   b. bilingual skills _____

   c. experience _____   d. a good attitude _____

Your Turn

In a small group look at newspaper want ads for one kind of job.
Write four things employers want. Make a bar graph.

VOCABULARY PROMPTS

In a small group talk about the words below.
Ask your teacher if your group doesn't know the word.

experience   volunteer work   respect

ISSUES AND ANSWERS

Read the letters below. Write a response to "Afraid."

Ask ABDUL and ANITA

DEAR ABDUL,

I am a student now. I don't have a job. In my country, I was a full-time student. Now, I want to apply for a job. What do I write on my job application about job experience? What do I say about job skills? Help!

NO EXPERIENCE

DEAR NO EXPERIENCE,

When I interviewed for my first job, I didn't have job experience. But I had experience helping my family. You probably helped your family too. Did you ever help with a family business? cook? clean? babysit? Volunteer work for relatives, school, or the community is experience. And you have at least one job skill—you can read, write, and communicate in two languages!

ABDUL

DEAR ANITA,

Sometimes I can't understand my boss. She speaks very fast. I'm afraid to ask her questions. I look at the floor and keep quiet to show respect. Sometimes she gets angry and says, "Look at me when I'm speaking to you!" I don't want to lose my job. Please help me.

AFRAID

DEAR AFRAID,

_____

_____

_____

_____

_____

ANITA

In your group talk about the letters to Abdul and Anita.
Talk about your answers to Afraid's problem. Are your answers
the same or different?

WRAP-UP

With a group of four finish the idea map about job interview questions. Ask and answer the questions. Now two students from your group go to another group. Two students from the other group come to your group. Practice asking and answering the questions again.

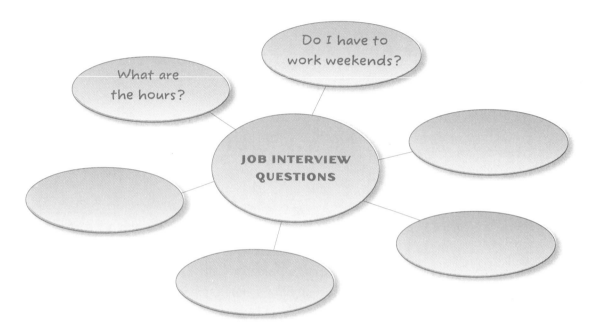

What are the hours?

Do I have to work weekends?

JOB INTERVIEW QUESTIONS

   ### Think About Learning

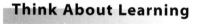 In this unit you learned a variety of skills and language structures. Look at the items in the list below and check how easy or difficult each item was for you. At the bottom write one other thing you learned.

SKILLS / STRUCTURES	Page	easy ☺	so-so 😐	difficult ☹
Talk about job interviews	97, 103			
Listen to conversations about jobs	98, 103			
Put together two sentences	100			
Read about job tips	101			
Read about a business person	102			
Use *can* and *can't*	99			
Understand a bar graph	106			
Read about problems and solve them	107			
Use an idea map	108			
Use *must*, *must not* and *have to*	104, 105			

UNIT 10 FINDING A BARGAIN

Talk about the pictures with a partner.
Ask each other the questions below.
Share your answers with another pair or the class.

Mei is talking to her friend Nicole about buying furniture.

FACTS   What's the problem? What does Mei want to buy?

FEELINGS   How does Mei feel about buying more furniture?
How does her friend feel about yard sales?

AND YOU?   Do you know about yard sales? Do you ever go to any?
Why or why not?

Before you listen, talk about the words below in small groups.

bargain   deliver   secondhand store   factory outlet   flea market

SOUND BITES

Mei's friends are telling her where she can get a bargain.

While You Listen Write the words from the list below to match the picture.

discount store   secondhand store   factory outlet
want ads   flea market   yard sale

1. _____

4. _____

2. _____

5. _____

3. _____

6. _____

After You Listen In small groups talk about yard sales, discount stores, secondhand stores, and want ads. Ask, "What is the best way for Mei to find a desk and chairs?" Discuss your answers.

In Your Experience

Ask and answer these questions in a group.

Where do you like to buy things?
Where did you find bargains in your native country?

SPOTLIGHT ON INDIRECT OBJECTS

Indirect object with *for*/*to*   OR   **Indirect object without *for*/*to***

Mei bought a table **for Tom**.   Mei bought **Tom** a table.

Mei bought a table **for him**.   Mei bought **him** a table.

They mailed the receipt **to Mei**.   They mailed **Mei** the receipt.

They mailed the receipt **to her**.   They mailed **her** the receipt.

Gary gave the book **to me/you**   Gary gave **me/you/him/her/us/them** the book.
    /him/her/us/them.

Indirect objects are nouns or pronouns. Use indirect objects to tell *whom* a thing
is done *for* or *to*. Use *for* or *to* when the indirect object is after the direct object.

Use *for* with these verbs: Use *to* with these verbs:

buy   order   send   give

make   cook   mail   take

find   get   show   write

Exercise 1: Complete the sentences. Use *for* or *to* as appropriate.

MEI: I bought some furniture (1) _____ you.

TOM: You did?

MEI: I bought a table and lamp (2) _____ you.
        I also ordered you four chairs.

TOM: Where are the chairs?

MEI: The store will send the chairs (3) _____ you tomorrow.

TOM: Who is this big pillow for?

MEI: That's not (4) _____ you. I got that pillow (5) _____ my sister.

Exercise 2: Now look at the sentences without *for* or *to* in the chart above.
Copy the story in your notebook, and use that word order.
For example, write, "Mei: I bought you some furniture."

In Your Experience

With a partner talk about presents you bought for people last year.
For example, say, "I bought a hat for Judy," or "I bought Judy a hat."

VOCABULARY PROMPTS

In small groups talk about the words and phrases below.

super   Wow!   Guess what!   really

Person to Person

Listen to these conversations about finding a bargain. With a partner, finish the last conversation. Use indirect objects if you can. Then practice the conversations with your partner.

MEI: I'd like to buy these chairs.
         Can you deliver them?

CLERK: Yes. We'll send the chairs to you tomorrow.

MEI: Super! Here's the address.

JUDY: What a beautiful jacket! I really like it.

NICOLE: I bought my friend this jacket and
         purse at a secondhand store.

JUDY: Wow! Can I go with you next time?

MEI: I found the perfect couch for you.

TOM: Where did you get it?

MEI: At a secondhand store. It was a bargain.

TANYA: Where were you?

MATT: At a yard sale. Guess what!
         I bought you a cute little table.

TANYA: _____

         _____

112   UNIT 10

VOCABULARY PROMPTS

In small groups talk about the words below.

compare	values	interest	payments
height	width	depth	credit card

READING FOR REAL

Mei is looking for a desk. She compares values in two newspaper ads.

Smull's Furniture Special
Computer Desk
Sale for 3 days only
Desks for computer use
Reg. $350 Sale $199
No interest, no payments
for 2 months

Shop at SavMart
Office Desk
$99.99
46" height x 29" width x 24" depth
Everyday Low Low Price
Ask a store clerk how you can save
up to 6% with a SavMart credit card.

Exercise 3: Circle the letter of the correct answer.

1. Which desk is less expensive?

   a. the computer desk   b. the office desk   c. both are the same price

2. Which desk don't you have to pay for now?

   a. the computer desk   b. the office desk   c. both

3. How much can you save on the computer desk?

   a. almost $20   b. over $150   c. nothing

4. What is the width of the office desk?

   a. 46″   b. 29″   c. 24″

5. How can you save with the office desk?

   a. use a credit card   b. buy in three days   c. buy now at a special low price

With the class decide which desk is a better value. Why?

Your Turn

Find two newspaper ads for the same product. Talk about them in a group.
How are they different? Which product is a better value?

CULTURE CORNER

SPECIAL
SAVINGS

At Mr. Pizza—**Save $2** when you order a large pizza.

SAVE MONEY WITH COUPONS

Do you want to save money? Use *coupons*—pieces of paper that give you discounts on things you buy. You can get discounts on drinks, pizza, frozen foods, office products, and other things. Usually you save 10 to 20 percent off the price. There are coupons everywhere in the United States. Here are some places to find them:

in the newspaper	in magazines	at your door
in the mail	in stores	

But be careful with coupons. Sometimes people buy something they don't really want because they have a coupon. Some products shown on coupons are even *more* expensive than other products!

Some people save a lot of money every year with coupons. Do you use coupons?

Your Turn

Write three questions about the reading on coupons.
For example, write, "What are coupons?" Then ask a partner the questions.
Write your partner's answers.

1. _____

2. _____

3. _____

In Your Experience

Talk about coupons in a small group.
Ask and answer these questions.

Do you use coupons?
Where do you find them?
What do you buy with coupons?
Which coupons do you like best?

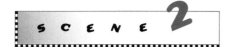

Talk about the pictures with a partner.
Ask each other the questions below.
Share your answers with another pair or the class.

Tom and Mei are at a discount store. They are shopping for a desk.

We could buy this desk. It has lots of space and drawers.

This desk is better. It costs less, and it's bigger.

Here's the desk for me! There's room for a computer. And it's cheaper, too. Only $59.90! What a bargain!

Guess what? The price is $599, not $59.90.

Too bad. I really liked that desk.

FACTS What's the problem? What are Tom and Mei doing?

FEELINGS How does Tom feel?

AND YOU? Do you compare values when you go shopping?

VOCABULARY PROMPTS

Before you listen, talk about these words in a small group.

drawers   expensive   comfortable   hole   item   refills

SOUND BITES

While You Listen Check the item the people like best.

1. wood desk _____   2. blue chair _____   3. $1200 computer _____

   metal desk _____   black chair _____ $1500 computer _____

After You Listen Check your answers with a partner.

SPOTLIGHT ON COMPARATIVE ADJECTIVES

Her lamp is small. My lamp is **smaller**.

The brown desk is big. The black desk is **bigger**.

This chair is **better than** the other chair.

Ken's garage is **dirtier than** our garage.

Their couch is **more expensive**.

Our computer is **less powerful** than Jack's.

big–bigger good–better dirty–dirtier expensive–more expensive

To compare things or people, add *-er* to most adjectives with one or two syllables.

For most adjectives with three or more syllables, use *more* or *less*.

Exercise 4: Mei and Tom are shopping. They are comparing two chairs. Use the words below to complete the sentences.

more comfortable   more expensive   better   smaller

TOM: Let's get the little wood chair. It's much (1) __better.__

MEI: But it's too hard. This big cloth chair is (2) _____.

TOM: But that chair is (3) _____. It costs $59.99.

And I like the (4) _____ wood chair.

Person to Person

Listen to these conversations about comparison shopping.
With a partner finish the last conversation.
Then practice the conversations with a partner.

SALES CLERK: I like this computer. It's more expensive,
but it's a much better machine.

MATT: How is it better?

SALES CLERK: This computer is faster and more powerful
than the others.

TOM: Let's buy the wood chair.

MEI: But the cloth chair is much nicer!

TOM: _____

_____

SPOTLIGHT ON *COULD*

Could has three meanings.

They **could** buy a new table next week, or they **could** buy a desk.
Use *could* to talk about future possibility.

Mei **couldn't** move the big couch yesterday, but Matt **could** move it.
Use *could* to show ability in the past.

Could you help us, please? **Could** I see the manager?
Use *could* for requests.

Exercise 5: Use *could* or *couldn't* to complete the story.

Nicole was moving to a new apartment. She moved the boxes,

but she (1) __couldn't__ move the big furniture. She told her friend

about the problem. (2) "_____ you give me some ideas?"

Laura answered, "Maybe one of our friends (3) _____ help."

Nicole called Jack, but he (4) _____ help. He had plans

on Saturday. She called another friend. "Hi, Matt. (5) _____

you help me move? I (6) _____ fix you a big dinner

as a reward." Matt (7) _____ already taste that dinner.

He said, "Sure. I (8) _____ come in the morning

or in the afternoon."

Exercise 6: Now look again at the different meanings of
could and *couldn't*. Mark each answer above as
A (ability in the past), **B** (requests), or **C** (future possibility).

In Your Experience

In small groups talk about next weekend.
Talk about two things you *could* do. For example, say,
"I could visit my friend, or I could go to a movie."
Then talk about two things you *couldn't* do.
For example, say, "I couldn't see Ana, because she lives far away."

VOCABULARY PROMPTS

Talk about the words below with a partner or a group.

fax machine   qualities   guarantee   office-supply store   decision

GET GRAPHIC

Tom needed a fax machine for his new shop. He looked for
the best value. He found information about each product.
Then he made a little chart so he could decide.

CHART OF FAX MACHINES

Location	Price	Qualities
Discount store	$385	New; one-year guarantee
Newspaper ad	$195	Used; no guarantee
Office-supply store	$489	New; two-year guarantee
Yard sale	$145	Used; no guarantee
Secondhand store	$245	Used; one-month guarantee
Flea market	$235	New; no guarantee

Exercise 7: Circle the correct answer.

1. The most expensive fax machine is from the

   a. newspaper ad.   b. discount store.   c. office-supply store.

2. The least expensive fax machine is from the

   a. newspaper ads.   b. yard sale.   c. flea market.

3. A machine that doesn't have a guarantee is from the

   a. newspaper ad.   b. discount store.   c. office-supply store.

Your Turn

In a group talk about which fax machine Tom should buy.
Share your answer with other groups. Give two reasons for your answer.

In Your Experience

Bring in the newspaper. Find ads for fax machines.
Make a comparison chart of this information.
Your teacher will help you.

VOCABULARY PROMPTS

Talk about the words below in a group.

debt   annual   fee

ISSUES AND ANSWERS

What happens if you don't have money to buy something?
Some people use a credit card. Tom and Mei need to buy more
things for their shop. They are thinking about using a credit card.
They wrote about reasons for and against using credit cards.
They want to know what could happen if they had a credit card.

FOR	AGAINST
We could buy things right away.	We could get into debt.
We wouldn't need to spend time looking for bargains.	We could buy more than we need.
We could buy more expensive products.	We could have trouble paying off the credit card.
We could pay the credit card bill later.	We could have to pay an annual fee.

Your Turn

In a group talk about the chart. Can you think of other reasons?
Then, in your group write one sentence with the best reason *for*
credit cards and one sentence with the best reason *against* them.
With the class, list all the groups' *for* and *against* sentences in a
chart on the board. Then cross out the repeated sentences.
Make a final *for* and *against* chart about credit cards with
all the reasons from the class.

WRAP-UP

Tom and Mei have a *budget*—a plan for saving and spending money.
They plan to spend an average of $200 a month to buy things for the office.
They also have a budget time line. A time line shows information in order
by dates. Write the items Tom and Mei could buy each month.

fax machine $250	bookcase $50	lamp $50
cabinet $75	4 chairs $50 each	fan $25
table $125	supplies $100	

MARCH	APRIL	MAY	JUNE	JULY
4 chairs				

Now write about Mei and Tom's time line in your notebook.
Use *could* in your writing. For example, write, "In March,
Tom and Mei could buy four chairs."

Think About Learning

In this unit you learned a variety of skills and language structures. Look at the
items in the list below and check how easy or difficult each item was for you.
At the bottom write one other thing you learned.

SKILLS / STRUCTURES	Page	easy ☺	so-so 😐	difficult ☹
Talk about people's problems	109, 115			
Learn about finding bargains	108			
Read ads	113			
Understand a time line	120			
Read about coupons	114			
Use a time line	120			
Use indirect objects	111			
Use comparative adjectives	116			
Use *could* and *couldn't*	117			

APPENDIX

COMMON IRREGULAR PAST VERBS

Base Form	Simple Past	Base Form	Simple Past
be	was, were	let	let
become	became	make	made
bite	bit	meet	met
break	broke	put	put
bring	brought	read	read
buy	bought	ride	rode
can	could	ring	rang
catch	caught	run	ran
come	come	say	said
cost	cost	see	saw
cut	cut	sell	sold
do	did	send	sent
draw	drew	set	set
drink	drank	sing	sang
drive	drove	shoot	shot
eat	ate	sit	sat
feed	fed	sleep	slept
fight	fought	speak	spoke
fly	flew	stand	stood
get	got	steal	stole
give	gave	swim	swam
go	went	take	took
grow	grew	teach	taught
have	had	tell	told
hear	heard	think	thought
hit	hit	throw	threw
hold	held	understand	understood
keep	kept	wear	wore
know	knew	win	won
leave	left	write	wrote

PRONOUNS

Subject Pronouns	I	you	he	she	it	we	they
Direct Object Pronouns	me	you	him	her	it	us	them
Indirect Object Pronouns (to / for)	me	you	him	her	it	us	them
Demonstrative Pronouns	this	that	these	those			

VERBS WITH *FOR* OR *TO* AND INDIRECT OBJECTS

Use *for* with these verbs:

buy (something) for someone
build
catch
choose
cook
find
get
keep
make
order

Use *to* with these verbs:

give (something) to someone
lend
mail
say
send
show
speak
teach
tell
write

COMMON COMPARATIVE ADJECTIVES

Comparative adjectives with one or two syllables usually end in *-er*.

tall	taller
short	shorter
long	longer

If the comparative adjective ends in *-y*, change it to *-i* before adding *-er*.

dirty	dirtier
pretty	prettier
ugly	uglier

Comparative adjectives with three or more syllables usually use *more*.

expensive	more expensive
beautiful	more beautiful
intelligent	more intelligent

Some comparative adjectives are irregular.

good	better
bad	worse